Object World

Christopher Bollas

Routledge
Taylor & Francis Group

LONDON AND NEW YORK

First published 2009 by Routledge
27 Church Road, Hove, East Sussex, BN3 2FA

Simultaneously published in the USA and Canada
by Routledge
270 Madison Avenue, New York, NY 10016

Routledge is an imprint of the Taylor & Francis Group, an Informa business

Typeset in New Century Schoolbook by Garfield Morgan,
Swansea, West Glamorgan
Printed and bound in Great Britain by TJ International Ltd
Padstow, Cornwall
Cover design by Andy Ward

British Library Cataloguing in Publication Data
A catalogue record for this book is available from the British Library

Library of Congress Cataloging-in-Publication Data
Bollas, Christopher.
  The ecovative object world / Christopher Bollas.
      p. cm.
  Includes bibliographical references and index.
  ISBN 978-0-415-47393-4 (hardback) – ISBN 978-0-415-47394-1 (pbk.)
1. Psychoanalysis. 2. Free association (Psychology) 3. Object
(Philosophy) – Psychological aspects. I. Title.
  BF175.B568 2009
  150.19'5–dc22

                                                            2008021170

ISBN: 978-0-415-47393-4 (hbk)
ISBN: 978-0-415-47394-1 (pbk)

Contents

Acknowledgements

The contents of this book were presented over an extensive period of time to two groups of psychoanalysts in Sweden. The essay on free association (Chapter 1) owes a great deal to years of collaboration with the Swedish Psychoanalytic Association (SPA). The chapter on architecture and the unconscious (Chapter 2) was delivered to the Stockholm Nationalmuseum and the Swedish Museum of Architecture in 1998 during the celebrations of Stockholm's year as European City of Culture. I want to thank the many members of the SPA and also its sister organisation, the Swedish Psychoanalytical Society, for their support over the last 30 years. Above all I wish to thank Dr Arne Jemstedt for his help in facilitating these meetings and for the remarkable generosity of spirit he has shown to all of us who took part. In addition he has read all my work and has provided invaluable insight that has changed the direction of my thinking in important ways.

I also want to thank the 30 people who have regularly attended the Arild Conference, on the shores of southern Sweden, every year since 1982. Their compassion for their patients and their unsparing honesty about their own work has been so refreshing and – if typically Swedish – is also a reason for every analyst in the world to visit Sweden at least once a year to recontact that passionate exploration which characterised the early years of psychoanalysis. I am grateful to Dr Ulla Bejerholm for her organisation of these conferences and for the care and affection with which she has received all of us who have attended.

Although *Free Association* (Cambridge, 2002) is no longer in print with Icon Books, I wish to thank them for publishing the original edition, as part of their Ideas in Psychoanalysis series. It appears here as Chapter 1 and has been revised for purposes of clarification. I am grateful to Taylor & Francis for permission to republish 'Architecture and the Unconscious', which first appeared in the *International Forum of Psychoanalysis* (vol. 9, 2000, pp. 28–42). Thanks also to Routledge for permission to republish 'The Fourth Object', which first appeared under the title 'Four: On Adding Up to a Family' in *Dimensions of Psychotherapy, Dimensions of Experience: Time, Space, Number and State of Mind*, edited by Michael Stadter and David E. Scharff (London & New York, 2005, pp. 165–180).

I want to thank my colleague Sarah Nettleton for her, as always, thoughtfully tough-minded and detailed comments on repeated drafts of this work. And my gratitude to Robert Timms for his skilful final edit.

Introduction

Freud's theory of how dreams are constructed has broad implications for the understanding of our mental life as a whole. His view that the stimuli for a dream arrive out of particular experiences during the day – those that he says are of 'high psychic value' – is predicated on an underlying assumption about the role of unconscious perception in everyday life.

What interests one dreamer will not be of interest to another, so these valued moments – we might call them emotional experiences – reflect the idiom of that self's unconscious life. In being moved by very particular events of the day we are revealed as seekers and interpreters of our own identity.

When we construct a dream we condense many of these experiences into single images. Further, this process of unconscious sorting involves contact with prior unconscious interests from the self's psychic history, so that our drives, memories, affects and existential axioms both assimilate and influence the quotidian.

Freud's method of free association was able to liberate in the dream not only the meaning of the prior day's events, but what the dream itself evoked in the mind of the dreamer. No dream could ever be interpreted completely, but Freud was content with the discovery of certain clear lines, or 'trains', of thought. Those lines – or 'chains of ideas' – were revealed through the course of listening to the analysand's free associations. The sequence of the associations in itself constituted a line of thought. If one listened long enough to this serial thinking, it was possible to see what was in the foreground of the self's mind, at least in that particular dream.

The first chapter of this book is an essay on free association. It is intended both as an introduction to the lay reader and as a reminder, or refresher course, for the clinician about the elementary foundations of Freud's theory of free association. I expand on Freud's concepts to illustrate how his theory of dream formation is actually a theory of the mind. (This essay was previously published by Icon Press; the version appearing as Chapter 1 of this book contains a number of revisions, especially in the section titled 'Affect, emotion, feeling'.)

The second chapter examines how the built landscapes in which we live reflect the unconscious nature of collective life, manifested in our buildings and cities. In walking through the world of actual objects we meander about in a world-daydream.

In Chapter 3 I review some aspects of my own theory of the 'evocative object' as it has evolved over 30 years, in order to set the stage for widening the concept of free association. We may extend the domain of the free associative to the world of actual objects, where the way we use them – and how they process us – is another form of the associative. There are many different ways to think; one way we think ourselves is through our engagement with, and use of, evocative objects.

The final chapter considers the phantom-like nature of that object we term a 'family'. If the number three in psychoanalysis signifies the Oedipal triangle, it does not necessarily announce the presence of a family. Indeed, as in Sophocles' *Oedipus the King*, the Oedipal triangle may destroy the possibility of this group becoming a family.

This book implicitly argues that there is no single place for 'the' unconscious. The old notion that one's mental life is 'unconsciously determined' is reductive and reactionary. It eliminates the many internal and external factors that contribute to any subject's unconscious life. Our articulations arrive unconsciously but they are sourced from thousands of localities over our lifetime.

Growing up *in* a family and *in* a city (or town, or village, or rural area) means that we become part of pre-existent unconscious formations. For Lacan the most significant 'import' was language itself, but we would certainly add the way our society dreams (which we term 'culture'); and at the other end of the spectrum of influence, we inherit genetic structures that influence the way we experience our lives.

Readers of this book may wish to know of its companion volume, *The Infinite Question*, published simultaneously. While *The Evocative Object World* introduces readers to core ideas, *The Infinite Question* develops them in greater depth, using clinical cases to illustrate the main concepts.

1

Free association

Riding the train

You are riding in a train, absorbed by the sights flying by. It passes an airport, crosses a canal, traverses a meadow, climbs a long, low hill graced by rows of vineyards, descends into a valley choked with industrial parks, winds its way through dark forests, and finally comes to the outskirts of the small city where you are to disembark.

Each location evokes sets of associations.

The airport reminds you of the coming summer and your holiday abroad. It recalls the plane that brought you to this part of the world in the first place; the never-ending expansions of airports; new aircraft on the design boards; the oddity of flight itself; and innumerable part-thoughts that almost enter consciousness but don't quite make it.

Crossing the canal, you think of a longed-for trip on a canal boat, yet to be accomplished, signifying the potential remainders of a life. You think of the Erie Canal in America and the songs and folklore linked to it. You think of your mother and father-in-law's former house which was alongside a small canal. You might also think of the dentist and a root canal.

And so it goes for the other 'objects' passed along this journey.

Freud used train travel as a model for his theory of free association: 'Act as though, for instance, you were a traveller sitting next to the window of a railway carriage and describing to someone inside the carriage the changing views which you see outside.'[1]

In a sense all Freud did was to take note of how when we think by not concentrating on anything in particular – moving from one idea to the next in an endless chain of associations – we create lines of thought, branching out in many different directions, revealing diverse unconscious interests.

For example, when electing a set of associations for the canal I came up with root canal work on one's teeth after describing the former location of one's in-laws: a line of thought I won't explore any further, but one which, were I to do so, might well divulge through the process of free association a much more complex story – a story revealed not between the lines, but in the chain of ideas within the lines.

Psychoanalysis concentrates on the daily 'trip' which we all take, stimulated by desire, need, memory and emotional life.

Trains of thought

The method of free association was designed to reveal a 'train of thought'. By just talking freely, any person reveals a line of thought – an Other line of thought[2] – linked by some hidden logic that connects seemingly disconnected ideas.

This is an ordinary part of everyday thinking. For example, I might start my walk to work thinking about a bill I must be sure to pay that afternoon when I'm at my office; then think about the rainfall and wonder if the sun will come out today; then think about a friend's newly published book which I haven't read and feel I should before we meet for dinner next week; then think about my early schooldays as I see children being dropped off at the nearby school; then think about how worried one could get as a child about being on time for school; then, on sight of a few sparrows flying by, think about the spring and wonder if they are now nesting; then think of the phrase 'nest eggs'. Here we may observe, in brief, the following chain: bills;

rainfall; friend's book; children dropped off; on time for school; birds nesting; and 'nest eggs'.

What do these ideas have to do with one another? Are they just random, or can we discern a train of thought?

I have a bill to pay and remind myself to pay it *later* that day. This is a kind of burden on my mind that may link with the rainy weather, itself burdensome: when will the sun shine? In other words, when will I be liberated from my burdens? Come to think of it, my unconscious seems to be saying, you also have another debt: you must read your friend's book before you meet for dinner. The sight of children being dropped off leads to a thought about being on time: a fear of being late may be an expression of my anxiety about paying the bill on time; simultaneously, by 'using' the sight of children to locate this anxiety, I am also likely to be taking refuge in the notion that a child such as myself should not have to pay bills. The sight of the birds, which I take to be parent birds building their nests, may sustain the appeal of a child being looked after, but the phrase 'nest egg' is probably a way of thinking about the bank and putting money away: building something for the future. Hopefully, I am on the way to living up to my parental responsibilities.

The Freudian Pair

Although he did not 'discover' free association, Freud's invention of the psychoanalytical session gave this ordinary way of thinking a highly privileged and utilitarian space. Most importantly, by asking the person to think out loud, he referred the monologist nature of solitary inner speech to the dialogic structure of a two-person relation, a partnership we might term the *Freudian Pair*. Let us see how he put it:

> The treatment is begun by the patient being required
> to put himself in the position of an attentive and
> dispassionate self-observer, merely to read off all the time
> the surface of his consciousness, and on the one hand to
> make a duty of the most complete honesty while on the

other not to hold back any idea from communication, even if (1) he feels that it is too disagreeable or if (2) he judges that it is nonsensical or (3) too unimportant or (4) irrelevant to what is being looked for. It is uniformly found that precisely those ideas which provoke these last-mentioned reactions are of particular value in discovering the forgotten material.[3]

Note that Freud does not give top priority to the disclosure of the disagreeable thought. The idea that the psycho-analyst is after one's dark secrets would not seem to be borne out by Freud's method. Instead, the most valued material is the apparently 'irrelevant'.

Freud believed that banished mental contents re-entered consciousness in thick disguise, and so it would be in the apparently trivial detail that forbidden ideas and emotions would more probably find expression.

The task assigned to the patient has been subject to various forms of misinterpretation. Did Freud really assume that anyone could disclose every thought passing through the mind? Indeed, would such a discourse not be rather bizarre? Almost immediately Freud qualified the injunction to speak the mind by indicating that there would be resist-ances to accomplishing this task, especially the arrival of the transference. But over time, psychoanalysts themselves seemed to change the meaning of free association into some form of ideal practice – so much so that by the 1950s it was common for analysts to say, sotto voce, that of course no one could do this. Even today, many analysts regard free associ-ation as a distant and unrealisable ideal.

Free talking

Matters come down to earth, however, if we redefine free association as *free talking*, as nothing more than talking about what is on the mind, moving from one topic to another in a freely moving sequence that does not follow an agenda. The analyst may encourage the patient to speak those thoughts at the back of the mind and, like Freud, will emphasise the need to interrupt a narrative if *other* thoughts arise; but even if patients rarely achieve this completely, they are nevertheless free associating if they move freely from one topic to the next in an hour.[4]

Embedded in such freedom of psychic movement are resistances to the return of previously repudiated ideas, as well as other defences against the mental pain derived from such freedom to think. Thus free association is always a 'compromise formation' between psychic truths and the self's effort to avoid the pain of such truths. Ironically enough, however, free talking always deploys the mental process of the analysand, revealing the struggle inherent to thinking one's self.

To patients in Freud's time and today, however, the method has often seemed almost wilfully indifferent to their plight. 'What, you mean, just tell you whatever is crossing my mind?' 'Can't you give me some sort of direction?' 'Well then, can't you ask me some questions, which I can answer?' 'But surely you have experience and know something of what I am suffering and what causes it – why don't you just explain it to me?' And often enough: 'Well I'm sorry, but I can't take this Freudian stuff. I have to go to someone who will really help me.'

Psychoanalysis does not provide ready answers to patients' symptoms or lives. Instead, it supplies a relationship that allows the analysand to hear from his or her own unconscious life, and Freud's insistence that the most valued material is to be found in the seemingly irrelevant – a kind of trivial pursuit – worked from modernist assumptions that to comprehend an object (a historical period, a novel, a person) one must study it in its ordinary sense, not pre-judged by hierarchical assumptions. If we see the belief in the quotidian as a valued source of human truth beginning in the Renaissance, continuing through Romanticism's privileging of ordinary human lives, and continuing to this day in those academic studies that believe everyday data is the primary object of scholarly research, then Freud's theory of evidence is the psychology of our times. Even the postmodernist tenet that any truth deconstructs into smaller truths – themselves disseminating through further epistemic declensions to fractions of their former assertions

– is an important outcome of the method of free association. In free associating to the dream, not only does the patient provide evidence that will enable the psychoanalyst to understand certain aspects of the dream; but as we shall see, the method also breaks up the unity of the dream into disparate lines of thought – which had been condensed by the dream-work in the first place – now disseminating possibilities that open to infinity.

The floating analyst

If the patient finds the task upending, what would he or she make of the psychoanalyst's job?

> Experience soon showed that the attitude which the analytic physician could most advantageously adopt was to surrender himself to his own unconscious mental activity, in a state of *evenly suspended attention*, to avoid so far as possible reflection and the construction of conscious expectations, not to try to fix anything he heard particularly in his memory, and by these means to catch the drift of the patient's unconscious with his own unconscious.[5]

This way of listening is revolutionary. The analyst is not meant to reflect on the material; not supposed to consciously construct ideas about the material; not encouraged to remember anything. And why? Because by surrendering to his or her own unconscious, the analyst is able to use it to 'catch the drift' of the patient's unconscious. In other words, psychoanalysis works through unconscious communication!

Any patient searching for an expert with answers would be even more disconcerted to discover how this 'mental health practitioner' works: caught in the act of drifting, what could the psychoanalyst say to the patient? Not much, it would seem. Indeed, the point of the analyst's task is to dissolve his or her own consciousness by not concentrating on anything, looking for anything, or remembering anything. Asking the analyst what he or she is thinking in the midst of listening to the patient would be akin to waking someone from a meditative state.

Freud's method was so disturbing that even his followers could not adhere to his explicit instructions and their implications. Instead, psychoanalysts have tended to focus on other parts of Freud's writings, especially on his view that psychoanalysis attempts to make unconscious conflicts conscious so that the patient has greater freedom of conscious deliberation. This is certainly true, up to a point. Through free association the psychoanalyst does indeed learn something about the patient's repressed views, and through moments of revelation – when the train of thought becomes suddenly clear in the analyst's mind – the psychoanalyst will disclose what he or she thinks he or she knows, adding perhaps to the patient's understanding of the self.

But the method has implications more wide-ranging than the already impressive accomplishment of rendering unconscious ideas to consciousness: it actually develops the patient's and the psychoanalyst's unconscious capabilities. This, as we shall see, is a new form of creativity fostered only in the psychoanalytical space.

Unconscious communication

'It is a very remarkable thing that the Ucs. of one human being can react upon that of another, without passing through the Cs.,' wrote Freud in 1915.[6] So, when the patient is free talking and the analyst is evenly suspended, the method becomes the medium for unconscious communication. Indeed, Freud had earlier likened unconscious communication to a telephone call, in which the receiver transforms the message into coherent speech. ('To put it in a formula: he must turn his own unconscious like a receptive organ towards the transmitting unconscious of the patient.'[7])

We might well puzzle about how exactly this transpires, especially as Freud – metaphors aside – does not spell out the terms of unconscious communication. Certainly he cannot be referring to his topographic model of repression, for if so, this would be a theory of self-deception through distortion: how could one person communicate his or her self-deceptions to the listening other, who, presumably, is functioning along similar lines?[8]

Let us search for clues in the Freudian Pair: the free associating analysand, the evenly suspended analyst.

A sequence of thought is revealed through a chain of seemingly unconnected ideas. A patient talks about listening to Bach's *Mass in B Minor*; then, after a pause, talks about going to Selfridges to buy a cricket bat for his son; then talks about a conversation with a friend in which the meaning of loyalty was the object of discussion; then talks about a memory from his youth when he found an abandoned car that proved to have been stolen a few days earlier, a topic the patient now realises is connected to a dream from the previous night; and so it goes . . .

What is the link between Bach/Mass and Selfridges/ cricket, and so on? Hard to tell, isn't it? If time permitted, we should just drift along with the patient's other associations until we reach a revelation – a point when suddenly we are struck by a pattern of thought, composed of those connecting threads between the disparate ideas.

Looking back, the logic of this brief sequence might reveal the following thought: 'I would be in a mess if as a consequence of my wish to enrich myself ["self-rich-es"] I did not play cricket [fairly] with my friends, especially if I were [car]ried off by stolen ideas abandoned by other people.'

Of course, this would inevitably be an incomplete understanding of the associations. Certain words, such as 'Selfridges', might call forth other words, so that in addition to the above we may also hear the words 'elf', 'rigid' or 'frigid'; the phrase 'that's not cricket' might be evoked, as might the multiple meanings of the word 'bat', in many differing contexts: 'right off the bat', 'old bat'. But even then, these signifiers meet potential other words on the rim of consciousness. Perhaps you can hear the word 'get' in 'cricket', or the word 'bad' in 'bat'. As the analysand free associates, presenting a field of sounds, the analyst will receive – mostly unconsciously – a complex tapestry of many connections.

There is, then, no single chain of thought: rather, as we shall see, multiple lines of psychic interest, moving through moments of life like some silent radiant intelligence. As the analyst assumes the position of evenly suspended attentiveness, he or she comes under the influence of the unconscious order. Guided by the logic of the patient's chain of ideas, the analyst at some point will retrospectively discover what the patient has, in part at least, been talking about.

The psychoanalyst's subjectivity

We communicate with one another unconsciously, therefore, when we give ourselves over to the way unconscious thinking takes place: through the free association of ideas that manifests a hidden order of thought. The psychoanalyst's unconscious recognises this as its own form of thinking and assumes the task of apprehending patterns of thought, some of which can be brought into consciousness.

But what about the psychoanalyst's own 'subjective response'? Would the analyst not distort what he or she hears? How could the analyst be relied upon to detect the chain of associations, given the dynamics of his or her own unconscious?

Confronted with the fact that the psychoanalyst will repress certain of the patient's contents, will condense various psychic materials into his or her own constellations of thought, will distort or alter communications according to the dream-work of the unconscious, how do we claim a capacity to discern, receive, integrate, and communicate with the patient's logic of association?

The problem is one of form versus content. The analyst's unconscious life will alter the patient's communications, dream-working them into unconscious complexes of the analyst's own creation; but at the same time the ego will follow the structure of the unconscious logic, a procedural capability unimpeded by the work of the analyst's own unconscious – much like operating a car is ordinarily uninfluenced by the driver's passing thoughts.

Pattern recognition is the ego's ability to perceive reality alongside the self's own unconscious contents or emotional states of mind. *If* the analysand thinks through free talking, therefore using the analyst as a medium for thought, then both participants use a part of the ego accustomed to the work of unconscious reception. Such reception begins in infancy, when the mother communicates complex messages to the infant through *forms* of behaviour – recurring patterns – assimilated by the infant as inner forms for processing lived experience.

The ability to follow the logic of sequence is a formal quality of the ego – a type of intelligence – not fundamentally influenced by the internal life of the recipient or the circumstances of the relationship between its participants.[9]

Indeed, in free dialogue, when two people free associate in the course of a long conversation, as is typical of close friends, they create unconscious lines of thought, working associatively, as they jump from one topic to the next. This is easy to do because we are open to such unconscious mutual influence when relaxed in the presence of an other.

Even as the analyst's unconscious tracks associative logic – doing nothing more than recognising the way we all naturally think – on other paths he or she will dream-work the patient's material: condensing words and images, substituting ideas; in other words, transforming the content according to his or her own unconscious reading. Later we shall discuss 'wavelengths' of communication, and how it is likely that the analyst's reception of the patient's material varies according to differing lines of evoked prior associations.

The analyst's unconscious knows where it is when 'in analysis', just as a composer's unconscious or a painter's unconscious knows the difference between that engagement peculiar to composing or painting and the many other moments in life, such as going to the bank or reading a book. Unconscious perception of the self's unconscious place is crucial to analyst and analysand knowing where they are and why they are there when they create psychoanalysis together.

At this point it is useful to introduce other factors that have contributed to the understanding and use of free association in contemporary psychoanalysis.

Object relations

Melanie Klein and her followers found that when we talk freely we often seem to be talking about parts of ourselves.

The patient free associates by using 'objects' to stand in for 'parts' of the self in relation to his or her mental objects, usually differing forms of representation of other people. So the chain Bach/Mass, Selfridges/cricket bat, friend/loyalty, youth/stolen car, etc., could be a free-moving drama in which differing parts of the self *objectify* a conflict in the theatre of free association. In this particular case we might say that the patient puts a solemn part of himself into the mass and then, made anxious by a partial realisation, proceeds to try to remove himself from this mental pain. A sequence of such interpretations might be as follows:

1   'You are listening to a depressed part of yourself.'
2   'You want to buy your way into being a game-playing boy to avoid your depression.'
3   'A part of you feels that leaving your depression behind is not a loyal thing to do.'
4   'You will find that such game-playing is just finding stolen solutions previously abandoned by you.'

Where Freud's way of listening takes a long time to discover a logic of sequence – entire sessions may be held in silence as a chain remains undiscovered – the object relational technique claims immediate meaning. If Freudian thinking holds that the manifest text never bears the unconscious but is only ever a thick disguise, then the object relational view accepts the manifest text as an accurate picture of parts of the self, even if what is being portrayed is open to question.

In fact, contemporary psychoanalysts tend to oscillate back and forth between these two listening perspectives, influenced by each.[10] Indeed, it is likely that the analysand uses differing forms of free association: from thinking as Freud saw it, according to the logic of sequence, to thinking as Klein saw it, according to the logic of projection. Thus in the same session a patient might suspend the sequential way of thinking in order to think through projection; equally, the analyst might move from listening in the Freudian manner to listening in the object relational manner.

Special effects

Object relations theory conceptualises another form of unconscious communication: that operating through the transference and the countertransference.

Patients think by acting upon the psychoanalyst; in this respect, talking is always a 'performative action' – to use J. L. Austin's term – as we have an implicit aim when we speak and we have differing effects on the other who listens. Of course, much of the time the action is benign: the patient is using the analyst's mind as a medium for free associative thinking. Sometimes, however, the patient's speech acts upon the analyst to gain some specific response, often a disturbed one.

Paula Heimann raised an interesting issue in the early 1950s when she asked of the free associating patient: 'Who is speaking, to whom, about what, and why now?'[11] Margaret Little, although she did not make an explicit connection, in effect asked a set of complementary questions: 'What am I feeling, about what, and why now?'[12] British psychoanalysts were to become deeply immersed in studying how the patient communicates his or her internal world through the wide range of effects he or she has on the analyst. In one case which attracted attention, for example, the patient always spoke in a very clipped voice whenever the analyst discussed the patient's feelings, the result being that the analyst felt hesitant to discuss the patient's emotional life. During one session the patient complained that he believed no one could feel what he was enduring in his life. The psychoanalyst said that he understood what the patient was talking about, explaining that he was reluctant to explore the patient's feelings because when he did, the patient became abrupt and dismissive. The patient found this meaningful, and said he believed that he didn't want anyone to take advantage of him when he was feeling vulnerable. The case led British psychoanalysts to an investigation of the unconscious anxieties and needs previously hidden within this form of transference.

Object relations theory helps us to see how one moment we might be speaking from our Oedipal self to a part of our mother's personality, then talking from our present age to a part of our own adolescent self, before talking to our self in its late twenties. In the course of a week of analysis we will be speaking not only from parts of our personality but also from parts of our mother or our father, each voice engaging some implicit or explicit other. Listen to the following patient at the beginning of an hour.

> Whew! What awful weather. I am *completely* worn out, feel like I'm dragging my feet. [*Laughs; then composes himself.*] So, down to work. So . . . what happened this last weekend? [*Pauses.*] Umm . . . I don't know really. Probably not much. Saw Frank, who as usual spent the weekend very productively [*etc.*].

The patient begins the hour talking like his mother, having internalised a dramatic, narcissistic part of her personality. He laughs as he did when he would describe her, but he is not conscious here that this laughter represents his amusement over the mother he has just presented. The sober enjoinment to get down to work is not simply a chip off the block of his father's voice. It brings this part of his personality into a typically paralysing position, resulting in the somewhat despairing comment that he does not know – a voice and a self state that was common for him as a latency-age child when admonished by his father. The Frank character is a projection of the patient's adolescent self – a self which typically resolved psychological and family issues by breaking out into great bursts of activity. Thus in the first few minutes of a session we can see the analysand speaking from several different parts of his personality, which are engaged in a form of intrapsychic dialogue with one another.

At times, free talking evokes a theatre of multiple selves and others immersed in a dense opera of identities 'thinking' about something through enactment. And usually such identities are simultaneously presenting various parts of the structure of the self's personality: a maternal part, an adolescent part, and an Oedipal part. So by free associating we sometimes release an intense discussion between the varying parts and functions of our personality, busy sorting out unconscious solutions to varied unconscious interests or conflicts.

Or, as discussed earlier, such parts can be elements of the self's personality engaging the analyst's diverse mental processes in a 'play of elements'.[13]

The discourse of character

A person's character is another type of free association. It bears assumptions about being and relating which cannot be thought about at first, but which are always divulged through the idiom of self-expression.

Character is self as form.

Think of a poem. A poem is enacted expression. 'Poems communicate before they are understood and the structure operates on, or inside, the reader even as the words infiltrate the consciousness,' writes Edward Hirsch. 'The form is the shape of the poem's understanding, its way of being in the world, and it is the form that structures our experience.'[14] Students of poetry (or music, or fine art) develop an unconscious sense of the formal identity of the objects they study, so that even if they have not previously read, heard or seen the specific object before them, they can often identify the writer, composer or artist from the immediate formal effects of the object. An end-of-year poetry exam, for instance, may involve 30 or more excerpts from as many poets' work, with the student having to match the name to the style.

So too with character. In ways even more complex than a poem, musical composition or work of fine art, we convey ourselves through action: we enact the idiom of our being through the way we shape the object world – an aesthetic motion that of course affects others. Indeed, the other shall 'know us' through this formal effect, in much the same way that Hirsch describes the operation of a poem upon the person reading it.

We could equally apply a musical metaphor, and say that character is a symphony of the self that uses the other as an instrument to play its idiom. Such employment, however, is only partially available for translation into consciousness. We may regard this aspect of free association as the movement of the 'unthought known': of something known about, indeed deeply informative of any self's being and relating, but something which must be experienced and can only meagrely be described.

This is *our otherness*.

As the movement of idiom conveyed by any self and experienced by its others, otherness both is and is not a property of each self: although it derives from the self, it can only be experienced by an other. Communication of our otherness is the path our being takes in, or through, life. A poem's style 'both creates the surface and calls upon – calls up – the deep unconscious life'[15] and in like manner so does the self's otherness. If others are open to any self's communication of its otherness – and of course there are many impediments to such reception, such as envy or hate – then the freedom of association that is the movement of character conjures up equivalent depths in the receptive others. As a form of communication in a psychoanalysis, character evokes depths of reception in the analyst – operating in the register of form, not of content – in turn eliciting deeper features of any individual's form in being. Patients often regress in an analysis, living out very early forms of being in what psychoanalysts term the pre-Oedipal or pre-verbal world. Such regressions can only occur if the analyst is open to the analysand's character, which inevitably expresses itself through thick movements of 'object use'. These movements operate before words are signifiers: they function in that world when wording was acting – when the word *was* the thing itself.

The Freudian Echo

Each generation of psychoanalysts returns to Freud, not simply to study the origins of psychoanalysis, but because his writings are so profound that one discovers a paragraph here or a sentence there that will provoke a rethinking of contemporary assumptions. It is an odd thing indeed – and for some quite embarrassing – to find on returning to Freud a future train of thought that was originally considered abandoned by him (probably for lack of time) and by his followers (probably for lack of genius).

Returning to the passage on the evenly suspended psychoanalyst, let us ask again: where would the psychoanalyst be while listening in this frame of mind, and how would one know if the psychoanalyst is communicating unconsciously with the patient?

In a sense, the answer is deceptively simple.

When listening to any patient free talking, the psychoanalyst will from time to time be struck by a certain word, image, body movement or turn of phrase. The psychoanalyst will not know why this is so; recall that the analyst is not meant to know why he or she is so moved. When the patient stops associating, often the analyst will find the patient's last word suggestive. 'I saw my colleague at the football match yesterday, and he was with a stranger.' Struck by the word 'stranger', the analyst echoes the word. If the analyst is in unconscious communication with the patient, then repeating an evocative word will sponsor further thoughts. In the case of the stranger, in fact, the patient not only talked about what the stranger looked like, he made a slip of the tongue and referred to 'the manger', the associations eventually leading to a fantasy that his colleague had been in the company of a figure who was the new Messiah of the business world.

By echoing the patient's words, a psychoanalyst surrenders to his or her emotional experience of the patient's discourse. This constitutes a working form of trust in the self's unconscious perception of the patient's communications, where the analyst can subsequently determine if he or she is in touch with the patient. If the patient is silent, or asks for a clarification, or is stilted in responding to the psychoanalyst's echo, this is usually evidence that the analyst has been out of touch with the patient.

The Freudian Mirror

The Freudian Echo is a form of mirroring: the psycho-analyst reflects the patient's discourse, transforming it from an 'ordinary' word embedded in the chain of ideas into something different. The word achieves a higher degree of psychic value, and now it resides in the patient's unconscious as a dynamic force (or 'node') that will attract related ideas and generate new meanings.

As a result of such mirroring, the patient's unconscious *senses* the presence of its counterpart in the other. It is as if a French-speaking person living in an English-speaking culture overhears (or subliminally hears) the analyst speaking French. Thus the patient can begin talking in French, hearing in return the desired language – or, we should say, the language of desire. For this aspect of the Freudian Pair, which opens up the discourse to the per-meability of unconscious thinking and influence, is almost certainly a form of desire peculiar to unconscious thinking. However, if the psychoanalyst does not listen in the Freudian manner, then we would have to say that the patient's unconscious may not perceive a counterpart and may not find its desire in the course of the analysis.

Slipping up

Free associating manifests the unconscious. It functions as an ever-sophisticated pathway for the articulation of unconscious ideas, regardless of their derivation: the logic of sequence; the logic of projection; the theatre of parts of the self talking to one another and to parental objects; or the movement of character.

Such increased accessibility facilitates a type of *porosity* as the analysand releases unconscious contents, often through an increased number of slips of the tongue. For example, in the midst of one analysis, a patient is hard at work both thinking about and trying to resist thoughts about her relation to her mother. The mother has always been carefully idealised by the analysand, but by now the patient is well into the capacity to free associate; so in one session when she says 'I shared a close emotional bomb with my mother', rather than the intended 'I shared a close emotional *bond* with my mother', the patient immediately senses the significance of her unconscious correction.

As the method of free association increases the porosity of speech – opening the self's discourse to this kind of parapraxis – it is almost as if the analysand's unconscious astutely grasps psychoanalysis as a kind of art form for its expression, and, having been frustrated in its desire to represent the self's true thoughts, rushes into the analytical space with a certain relish.

, Free talking is its own form of thinking. By 'thinking out loud', the patient discovers what they didn't think they knew, yet they also find in this form of representation a new technique for thinking. Ironically enough, the aspersion 'you don't know what you are talking about' becomes a stunningly positive quality in a psychoanalysis, where the analysand learns just that. Indeed they *don't* know what they are talking about, but such liberation therefore allows them to discover that the unconscious talks through the self's consciousness and, looking back, can retrospectively be comprehended from time to time.

Importantly, patients find a discourse that allows them both to free the unconscious mind and to hear from it. Analysands 'into' free association are also listening to the flow of ideas; this intra-subjective object relation (part of subject relations[16]) develops for each person a radical and entirely new relation towards the self. Were the psychoanalyst to be the sole interpreter of a patient's discourse, the possibility of this new form of being (with oneself) would be destroyed. Fortunately, however, analysts steeped in Freud's theory of technique know that one of the great accomplishments of psychoanalysis is the patient's newfound relation to his or her own unconscious life.

Faith and objectivity

The stereotypical portrayal of the Freudian analyst is a rather authoritarian individual with a powerful set of established truths, just waiting for the right moment to indoctrinate the patient in the Freudian ideology. If it is something of a relief to find that this is not so, it may also constitute an ironic disappointment. In reality, psychoanalysts who work within the Freudian Pair do not know for very long periods of time what their patients mean by what they say. Hardly in a position to have an idea-in-waiting for delivery, the Freudian psychoanalyst is genuinely lost in the movement of the patient's communications. It takes considerable self-discipline and faith to adhere to this way of listening.

Nevertheless, wouldn't the psychoanalyst be able to offer points of view and personal doctrines?

Any one person listening to any other person can always offer prescriptive advice, including recommendations to follow the listener's ideological edicts. And were the psychoanalyst inclined to do so, he or she could step outside the Freudian Pair to do the same as anyone else. Clearly Freud stepped outside his own method frequently enough to advise patients and to instruct them in one or other of his views of human conflict. Indeed, we may expect that psychoanalysis as a theory of conflict is inevitably saturated in predetermined ideas imparted from analyst to patient. This is a criticism of psychoanalysis that any of its detractors can immediately suggest, because they know from their own personalities that any self comes with its dogmas. So what is there in psychoanalysis to offset this unfortunate universal trait?

The method of free association subverts the psychoanalyst's natural authoritarian tendencies as well as the patient's wish to be dominated by the other's knowledge. This is all the more reason, then, to reflect on the extraordinary wisdom of a method which demands that the analyst dispense with his or her conscious memories and intentions, instead to surrender to a form of listening that actively dispossesses the analyst of the ability to impart his or her own ideology – Freudian or otherwise. Instead, the analyst is left with Freudian faith: a belief that if one gets rid of oneself (and all one's theories) and surrenders to one's own emotional experiences, then eventually the patient's unconscious thought will reveal itself.

Freud used the word 'faith' to describe the frame of mind one needed to take part in his method:

> I know that it is asking a great deal, not only of the patient but also of the doctor, to expect them to give up their conscious purposive aims which, in spite of everything, still seems to us 'accidental'. But I can answer for it that one is rewarded every time one resolves to have faith in one's own theoretical principles, and prevails upon oneself not to dispute the guidance of the unconscious in establishing connecting links.[17]

Freudian faith is supported by the analyst's intuitive intelligence that reflects his or her unconscious receptivity. Echoing the patient's comments purely from one's own *sense* of the patient's unconscious work is highly productive. Quite literally, this echo produces more material from the patient and in this sense is highly objective (it produces *more* mental objects). A deep intersubjectivity yields its own form of objectivity.

By suspending personal views and psychoanalytical theories in order to support the patient's unconscious thinking, the psychoanalyst not only facilitates the production of more thought, but he or she also assists the patient in establishing the truths of the patient's own analysis. The patient will be the author of his or her own meaning. It will be the patient, not the analyst, who supplies the psychoanalysis with fields of significance, creating a complex tapestry of associations that become deeply informative.

Meshwork and the receptive unconscious

Freud believed that the unconscious was capable of development ('the Ucs. is alive and capable of development . . . [and] is accessible to the impressions of life').[18] In the dream book he provides a clue as to how such development takes place:

> The dream thoughts to which we are led by interpretation cannot, from the nature of things, have any definite

endings; they are bound to branch out in every direction into the intricate network of our world of thought. It is at some point where this meshwork is particularly close that the dream-wish grows up, like a mushroom out of its mycelium.[19]

'Meshwork' is James Strachey's translation of the German word *Geflecht*, which also means 'network' or 'wickerwork'. This 'branching out' occurs through the analysand's free associations: in the course of an analysis, the patient's branches develop into a network of thought that constitutes the matrix of the analysand's unconscious as it functions within the psychoanalytical space. By asking for free associations and by receiving them through a very particular frame of mind, the psychoanalyst not only increases the network of knowledge but also, simultaneously, enhances the patient's unconscious reach.

The psychoanalyst develops the patient's unconscious capability.

To use Winnicott's theory of the true and false self – a distinction he made in the first place to discuss the compliant person who abandoned his or her own intrinsic desires and beliefs in order to suit the demands of the other – we can see how the Freudian Pair facilitates the articulation of the analysand's true self. By 'true self' we do not mean 'true' as an absolute, or even 'true' in the purist sense of comparison to the false self, as the latter is also a true part of a person's character. Winnicott meant that any person's true self was the spontaneous gesture – in being, playing, speech or relating – that was evidence of the self's momentary expression of the desire to present or to represent the self's particular idiom. By stretching, yawning, or looking at an object while conversing with another, the self may break the moment's convention. Such movements are signs of the spontaneous.

True self is the freedom of the self's idiom to realise itself in the forms of everyday living, while false self refers to the self's adoption of forms that restrict this freedom.

The Freudian Pair suspends average expectable compliance. Of course, it could be argued that the analysand does indeed comply with the injunction to free associate, and certainly Freud was at times very insistent that the patient accept this demand, so it is clear that the rule is a paradoxical one. The patient is to adapt to a medium that fosters the articulation of the unconscious: he or she succumbs to freedom of speech.

Free to speak whatever crosses the mind, the Freudian analysand gradually grows accustomed to moving from one topic to another, as events of the previous day, dream reports, self observations, memories and the average interests of everyday life come to mind in the analytical session. No patient says everything, but Freud did not expect an absolute report. All patients keep secrets, whether memories of differing forms of indiscretion, sexual ideas that seem too private to disclose, or former actions which haunt the self with guilt. What matters in Freudian practice is that the analysand keeps talking, moving from topic to topic, without (consciously) trying to figure out what it all means, and tolerating the comparative absence of analytical comment.

After a while, patient and psychoanalyst find their own way with the method. Subtle variations arise. The patient will often be silent, engaged in deep associative thought which will *not* be reported. The psychoanalyst will also have many associations to what the patient says which will go undisclosed. Often the psychoanalyst will find that when he or she is making a comment the patient appears to have drifted off. The analyst discovers that his or her interpretation is used not for its apparent accuracy, but as a kind of evocative form: because the analyst is talking, curiously the patient is free not to listen! But in not listening, the patient seems intrapsychically directed towards another interpretation. To the analyst's observation 'You are thinking of something else?', the patient replies that as the analyst was speaking the patient was thinking of x, where x might be an interpretation from the analysand's unconscious that will be different from the analyst's; but x will not have been possible without the analyst's interpretation constituting difference in that moment.

Freud's theory of meshwork also enables us to expand further our understanding of the analyst's unconscious comprehension of the patient's communications. All along, of course, while in the state of evenly suspended attentiveness the psychoanalyst is engaged in his or her own inner free associations to the patient's material. As discussed, the analyst will often be struck by a particular word or image and on occasion will echo it, an act solely determined by the analyst's own pre-associative sense of the value of the word. But in time the psychoanalyst will have woven a vast network of inner associations built around the patient's communications; and that network will become the psychic field through which the analyst filters the ongoing history of the patient-in-analysis.

Repression or reception?

Both participants are engaged in unconscious work, but the co-operation accomplished in the Freudian Pair offers a complementary notion of the unconscious to the one which Freud privileged. Freud emphasised the repressed unconscious in his effort to discuss the mental fate of unwanted ideas. In 1923, however, he was struck by what seemed to be a contradiction in this theory of the unconscious.[20] In addition to the existence of repressed contents, there was also an agency of the mind performing the repression that was itself unconscious. What was he to do with these two different definitions of the unconscious?

Freud never formally resolved this problem, but it is easy enough to find in his writing a tacit resolution of the apparent contradiction. The agency of repression is of course the ego, which operates the mechanisms of the mind. It is the ego which conducts the dream-work, which forms symptoms, which stores psychically valuable moments during the day, which organises any and all features of a self's unconscious life. The ego has a vested interest in perceiving reality, in giving it organisation, and in communicating it to others. If in the beginning of the human race such organisation was essential to human survival, in less dire circumstances it became a form of pleasure in its own right. And while repression of unwanted ideas is a necessary defence against unpleasant feelings derived from those ideas, reception of reality is a necessary condition to the self's survival and pleasure.

Freud did not formally create a theory of the receptive unconscious in contradistinction to the repressed unconscious, but his theory of dreams and his belief in and use of unconscious communication reveal a complex assumption about the ego's receptive capability (and the return of the received) in the many different forms of communication, whether in speech, painting, composing or moving the body.

Psychic genera

Any self receives and alters reality, organising life into memory banks (or meshworks) where perceptions nucleate in highly condensed psychic matrices.

Life interests us in many different ways. Curious to begin with, our desire seeks its pleasure through countless gratifying moments, memorable to varying degrees. Psychoanalysis is a theory of memory's desire: of experiences that, having yielded a certain value, become the basis of subsequent related interests. Over time a self organises thousands of interests (and their history) into psychic areas that make possible differing new perspectives on the self's vision of reality.

Such mental structures begin as questions derived from simple experiences. 'How can I gain this pleasure again?' 'How do I avoid further pain of that kind?' 'What is this which interests me?' Such questions are referred by the unconscious to different psychic locations at work on related issues. In the beginning of life, for example, the breast is an object of desire. 'What is this?' forms the paradigm of all questions, and any self will organise a psychic structure around desire and its history that will not only drive further curiosity but also sponsor important mental realisations, or epiphanies, that develop the self.

A patient, for example, has for months been unconsciously working on issues that seem to have something to do with colour and light. One week he talks about painting a room; another week this theme recurs in the topic of the lighting of objects that he considers undertaking as part of a professional project; and another week he has a series of dreams that, in part, portray interests in the colour of skin. One day he arrives for a session having passed by a bakery, where he noted the pale opacity of a type of French bread. He felt he was in the quiet before a revelation, and in the session, while talking about the summer holiday to come, he said: 'I think I would like to go to Tucson.' He had thought of Tucson before, but had never experienced an urge to go there. In a series of fast-moving associations – more like the formation of a realisation – the patient quickly linked up the colours of the desert with different types of plant and animal life indigenous to Arizona. He then remembered a woman from his childhood called 'Tucson Peg', a woman he knew only as a close friend of his parents, as she visited the family every summer for a few days. Out of this complex of ideas the patient suddenly said: 'I remember one day being very attracted to my mother, finding her incredibly beautiful in her bathing costume. I realise that I have declined to follow anything associated with her beauty because it is forbidden.'

How do the prior associations *add up to* this realisation? We shall not know. We can infer that the patient's increased interest in colour had something to do with the beauty of his mother, for after this session he was more specific, recalling the colour of her costume and her beautiful skin. He also recalled a painting in the house – a colourful portrait of a woman – which he had always had very special feelings toward. He remembered finding Tucson Peg a very attractive woman. And Tucson itself he associated with the freedom and the beauty of the West.

We can see, then, the patient working for several months on what we may term psychic genera[21] – gathering impressions into one area of the self's psychic life – in order to assemble the mental material of what would ultimately be a new perspective on himself, his past, and his future. Such internal constellations of interest form through the associations of thought during the day, usually in response to discrete episodes of lived experience, following long-standing desires in the self. When the structure reaches an epiphany, understood here as a moment of insight that allows the self to increase its reflective capacity, the person looks upon himself and others in a somewhat new manner.

One of the intriguing features of an analysis is the fact that patients have these organised inner compositions which, like magnets, attract further impressions and serve as the core of the self's creative articulation of the inner compositions themselves. Psychic genera receive the impressions of life, sponsor new perspectives on the self's existence, and at the same time drive to represent them in being, playing or relating.

Genera reflect the work of reception, which follows the self's epistemophilic instinct: the wish to know. Working on knowing is a form of pleasure, derived in the beginning from the infant's exploration of the mother's body (real or imagined) and the child's Oedipal lusts. The work of reception is also driven by the ego's desire for mastery (of its psychic reality) expressed through its organisation of the impressions of life. Areas of interest are collated and stored in the unconscious until such time that they may generate a new perspective, at which point there is some form of emotional recognition of the presence of a new-found insight.

The work of reception can be distinguished from the work of repression in that reception is the desire to receive and organise impressions in order to have deeper access to the pleasures of life, while repression reflects the work of anxiety, which banishes impressions disagreeable to consciousness. Receptive organisations, however, are open to repressed phenomena. In the example above, it is clear that the figure of Tucson Peg is derived partly from repressed desires for the patient's mother.

Psychoanalysts appreciate that patients seem to be engaged in different unconscious works. At any one time in an analysis, a patient is developing innumerable unconscious compositions. While talking about issues in his or her life, the patient reveals unconscious selection driven by the desire of each composition; and free associating works on these compositions. Unconsciously receptive to the patient's communication, the psychoanalyst too engages in the work of composition.

If repression seeks to banish the unwanted, reception gathers the desired. Whatever the nature of the content, the ego has many means at its disposal for the differentiated placement of pleasure and unpleasure within the differing nuclei that constitute the matrix of the unconscious. Outside the analysis it does this on a small scale throughout the day, when it organises the interests of the day into the dream that night. We can use this as the paradigm of psychic genera. The concerns of the day, which in turn are linked to the self's total history up until that point, gather into pressure groups that will urge the ego to form dreams that night. These gathering points are psychic genera which desire organisational mastery in order to achieve the pleasure of representation.

To some considerable extent, Freud provided a theory of what are here termed 'genera' in his concept of 'nodal points'. He believed that psychic life was concentrically stratified, with diverse logical threads emanating from, or drawing towards, psychic nuclei along 'an irregular and twisting path', and – crucially – that 'this arrangement has a dynamic character'.[22] He then adds:

> The logical chain corresponds not only to a zig-zag, twisted line, but rather to a ramifying system of lines and more particularly to a converging one. It contains nodal points at which two or more threads meet and thereafter proceed as one; and as a rule several threads which run independently, or which are connected at various points by side-paths, debouch into the nucleus.[23]

These nodal points are genera. They come together from diverse sources that find in a momentary network some form of shared interest that now becomes 'overdetermined' – an interest now more forceful than before which, amongst other consequences, will demand representation.

Questions of the day

The curious laboratory of psychoanalysis allows us to see how people think unconsciously. Most commonly a session seems to pose implicit or explicit questions. A patient may begin with a gripe about some aspect of life, perhaps a statement such as: 'I hate it when people don't respond to traffic signals.' This declaration gradually breaks down into the question 'Why do I hate it when others don't respond to traffic signals?', which on further association deconstructs into multiple questions. The 'traffic signal' may divide into 'traffic' and 'signal', the word 'traffic' leading eventually to the patient's anxiety about his daughter spending time with people trafficking in drugs. For a while the word 'signal' may linger, connected to this anxiety, as the patient comes to ask, in effect, if he heeded the signals displayed by the daughter. Eventually that word may diffuse into 'single', 'signs' and 'sighs', and from there into 'sights' and further 'si-' sounds that disperse the condensations held by that signifier. So what begins as a statement quite naturally leads to diverse questions, which in turn metamorphose into other questions, under the mutative spell of free association.

Patients often surprise themselves with quite explicit questions and – most interestingly – they will frequently supply an unconscious answer. Talking about his anxiety over visiting an uncle, a patient says: 'I don't know why I'm worried about visiting him.' He pauses, says, 'Oh well', and then goes on to talk about something that would seem to be completely different. 'I was out with my friend Alice. We went to this restaurant, and you know, I'd forgotten just how loud she can become when she starts to talk about her former boyfriend. My God it was embarrassing.' Following the logic of this association, the psychoanalyst might very well say something like: 'You asked why you are worried about visiting your uncle. Is your association an answer: are you afraid he will embarrass you?'

Chances are this is true: the logic of association is a form of unconscious thinking, so if the patient asks a direct question, pauses for a moment, and then proceeds to talk about something else, it is most likely that the next topic is some form of answer.

It is not long before the analysand begins to appreciate associative thought. After all, the material used by the analyst will have come, in this respect, entirely from the patient. The source of truth, such as it is, will have been derived from the analysand's process of thought. Yet the implications of this form of work are wide-ranging and most intriguing.

Wavelengths

When people talk about communication with one another, they may refer to 'being on the same wavelength'. We may observe something of this notion in psychoanalysis when we examine the 'frequency' of a patient's associations. Freud focuses on the logic of sequence in the here and now, a logic that ultimately reveals some close reading on the patient's part of his or her lived experience. But the analyst will also note certain words, images, memories, dreams and prior patterns of thought recurring across sessions. Indeed, it may become clear that a patient discussing the *QE II* liner and the price of a ticket to New York may have had a dream about being on board a ship two weeks before, which in turn linked to his memory of travelling to Santander on a large car-ferry.

Some patterns of free association seem to have large frequency intervals, the line of thought articulating itself over a longer time-span than the more domestic work of the immediate associative logic of the hour. Sometimes particularly vivid and emotionally moving dreams condense issues worked on by the self over a long period of time.

This should come as no surprise.

During the day certain people, places and events have more emotional effect on a person than others and their psychic value will compete to form a dream that night. But such experiences will often possess such value because they fall circumstantially into the path of a prior interest which is now in the process of disseminative movement. Each line of interest is always finding something in lived experience that gathers magnetically to it, forming thousands and thousands of nuclear interests. The patient dreams – often making new links between prior interests – and then the new day comes, during which the dream and its many aspects break up under new free associations and aleatory events in the real.

The free associating patient, however, will carry on thinking ideas that have been around since childhood, many of which have very long wavelengths, some taking years to recur. It may be years before a recurring dream returns, but its repetition speaks to one particular line of thought, sustaining its interests throughout the life of the self.

The Freudian Pair constitutes a mixed sequential temporality. Although the session is part of some more local interest and binds many prior interests into a shared space for a while, it is also a temporal collage, as lines of thought pursued in many different temporal rhythms are present at the same time. The psychoanalyst's open-mindedness allows the psychoanalyst to be under the influence of any wave of thought, whatever its frequency. Indeed, the analyst may unconsciously perceive a line of thought which arises momentarily, but whose history long precedes the analysis, removing it from any possibility of translation into consciousness.

Does the psychoanalyst possess a temporal capacity that can operate on varying wavelengths? The repetition of clusters of association, occurring in differing temporalities, instructs the analyst's unconscious as to the wavelength of that network. Indeed, if it is the case that approximately every three weeks an analysand talks about her relation to her father, then we may assume that every three weeks the analyst's unconscious will have tuned in to that wavelength.

Clearly, certain events in life occur at regular intervals. A payslip at the end of the month will always bring up some material about what to do with money. The months of the year bear cultural significance releasing sets of associations, as do particular days such as Christmas, Easter, New Year's Day, and so forth. The analysand's birthday, the date of the mother's or father's death, the date when the patient moved from one country to another; all occur at regular intervals and will bring up sets of associations. But human lives have much more precise and dense psychic calendars that make for repetition and create intervals that will not be consciously clear to the patient or to the analyst. Does the patient remember that it was on 5 April 1951 that her mother ran over another child in the family car? Or that on 14 October 1953 the father lost his job? Or that on 22 February 1956 the patient's mother miscarried? It is unlikely that these days will be consciously remembered by the analysand, but they will have been stored in the unconscious; and when each date occurs in the annual calendar it could evoke unconscious memories linked to all those significant prior events in the individual's life. Indeed, it is often by a recurrence of mood that the analyst will discover something quite forgotten. For example, after working with a patient for three years it was clear that every April the patient became depressed. Only when asking the patient if anything upsetting had ever happened in April did the analyst learn that this was the month when the patient's mother committed suicide. It was possible to observe from the Aprils which followed that the same thing occurred. What is unusual about this moment is that it enabled the analyst to discover the agency of the interval; ordinarily, he or she may not learn the significance of such intervals, or even be aware that a wave occurs every year at the same time.

To make matters more complex – but more accurate – we can say that these different waves of unconscious interest, which permeate any period of free associating, overlap with one another to form the symphonic movement of the unconscious. A patient sees a car accident the night before a session, and as she reports this event it will have activated another set of associations linked to the occasion when her mother ran over a child in 1951. Those will not be the only interests in the analytic hour, as there will be other emotional experiences of the previous day, dreams from the night, and associations before the session that will have nucleated into separate areas of interest. But all these

interests do become part of the same moment in unconscious time, and they are all shaped by the patient's ego
into the dream-work of ordinary free associating, in which
the patient moves from one topic to the next, quite ignorant
of all that he or she is processing in the here and now.

We may well find that, correspondingly, the listening
analyst has something in common with the musical audi-
ence. For this is an action that demands the ability to follow
disparate representations – some repeated, others quite
new – occurring at the same moment in time.

The drive to represent

Freud was never able to answer the question that he
continually posed to himself: isn't every dream a wish
fulfilment?

He found dreams that seemed to be beyond the human
wish.

Freud's error was to confuse mental content with
mental form. He tended to restrict himself to examination
of specific mental contents – anxiety dreams, and so on –
which challenged him to find the hidden wish in what
would otherwise seem to be a highly unpleasant activity of
mind.

What he failed to see was something quite simple: any
dream fulfils the wish to dream – thus every dream is a
wish fulfilment.

The dream is a *form* of unconscious representation.

By likening the dream to a symptom, Freud noted that
the ego picked differing forms for the representation of
unconscious contents. Because he failed to appreciate this
human wish to represent, Freud could not attend to the
underlying drive of the ego and to many of the issues that
explain unconscious communication. His theory of the
instincts came close; but it is not the case – as the classical
school was to argue – that all human thought is a collation
of derived individual instincts. This is a theory of content
gone too far, and it confuses form with content.

The infantile instinct – an intrapsychic arc from its
source to its object – is a paradigm of representation. To

satisfy the instinct, the self must construct an object. Putting it simply: if the instinct is the drive of hunger, then the object would be the thought 'I am hungry' or an image of something to eat. This is repeated throughout infancy and childhood, and although the infantile paradigm does not constitute the character of all individual instincts per se, it always generates the drive to represent the self.

The representational drive is what makes the human being uniquely human.

The desire to represent the self presupposes the self's belief in a good object, which in turn is based on the self's communications of early infantile states to the mother who, to lesser or greater extent, has received and transformed those communications. We may think of the pleasure of this representation and its reception as superseding the pain of any particular represented content. Thus the pleasure principle of representation drives the self to communicate with the other, and part of this complex action is the self's unconscious investment in seeking its own truth.

Seeking one's truth

What would it mean to seek one's own truth?

It could only ever mean seeking to represent unconscious conflicts in order that the representative process in itself might begin to undertake the task of self-liberation. The pleasure of representation promotes other pleasures: the pleasure of self-discovery, and of being understood.

Turning to the Freudian Pair, we may now see how the free associative process continuously gratifies the self's pleasure in representation, especially as it serves the drive to represent the self's unconscious interests. The analyst, in a state of even suspension – unintrusive, concentrating, receptive, dreamy – derives this presentational craft from the constituents of maternal creativity. And just as the mother receives and transforms her infant's communications, conveying through each moment of maternal care a type of devotion to the development of the infant's idiom, so the psychoanalyst's function within the maternal order effectively elicits the analysand's presentation of idiom for further articulation.

Free association within the analytical relationship differs from the ordinary associations of everyday life due to the process of speaking oneself in the presence of the other. The analyst's maternity, as it were, celebrates this type of communication and the analysand's 'speech acts' reflect the movement of the self as a form in being. Patients free associating are akin in this respect to artists manifesting a deeply subjective style through the form of their representation, much like a poet's signature is revealed not through the poem's content message, but through its form.

This form of reception is surely what Winnicott had in mind when he likened the psychoanalyst's concentration to 'holding'. Bion also points toward this aspect of the psychoanalytical relationship when he refers to the analyst as 'containing' the patient. Indeed, Bion enjoins the analyst to be 'without memory and desire', essential if the analyst is to achieve a very special state of mind he calls 'reverie'. By 'holding' the patient through 'reverie' the psychoanalyst receives the patient's unconscious moves, which will not only yield more information about the patient's inner life and historical conflicts, but will facilitate the articulation of the analysand's being, as a form of expression.

We may now add a further dimension to our understanding of how free association facilitates unconscious communication. By taking in the patient's being-as-form – operationally imparted not just by the logic of the patient's associations, but also by the shape created by the speech acts – the psychoanalyst is internally structured by the 'language of character'.[24] Over time, the psychoanalyst becomes familiar with each patient's being-as-form and can unconsciously read increasingly typical features of the analysand's style. It is very likely that this 'language training' accounts for the many moments in an analysis when, quite uncannily, the psychoanalyst either seems to know what the patient is going to say next (often supplying the next word) or, on the basis of a mix of verbal association, body gesture and mood, to 'feel' the patient's meaning.

Mind expansion

As free association produces further 'spoken objects', over time it establishes a meshwork for the Freudian Pair, and eventually creates an unconsciously comprehensible language of the analysand. More often, the psychoanalyst's passing comments are echoes of words or phrases that have moved the psychoanalyst, derived no doubt from his or her own unconscious collaboration with the patient. The to-and-fro implicit in this method becomes a new form of thinking, and both gathers together the psychic intensities of the patient's life – from dreams, clusters of association, images, memories – and breaks them apart as these momentary organisations disseminate upon further association.

By the middle period of a psychoanalysis the patient will have a substantially increased ability to think the unconscious. Moreover, he or she will have been participant in a form of unconscious relating that will have enhanced the self's capacity to receive, organise, create, and communicate with the other. All persons form mental representations of the other, in the form of internal objects. Psychoanalysis not only favours the representation of such objects, it also facilitates the self's capacity to communicate the aesthetic of its being to the other. It allows the self to convey its own otherness.

In a sense, this accomplishment of psychoanalysis has less to do with facilitating change per se as with *receiving* the analysand. And the efficacious outcome of an analysis may well be, in large part, the deeply meaningful experience one finds in conveying one's self to an other: perhaps fulfilling a need latent for thousands of years in our species, only now finding a form that has evolved to suit this need.

As the analysand develops the capacity to think, communicate and receive at these unconscious levels, we may say that psychoanalysis assists in the growth of the patient's mind. Although that expansion will include consciousness – both participants are conscious recipients of the effects of the unconscious work – the greater gain will be in the development of unconscious capabilities.

Indeed the association of ideas, or meshwork, is the unconscious. Thoughts, said Bion, require a thinker: the mind derives from the requirement to think nascent thoughts. In like manner, the self's history of associated ideas not only represents particular psychic interests, it also leaves a dynamic trace of connections that serve to perceive subsequent 'realities' from increasing depth. The course of associations sets up psychic patterns of interest which, once established, constitute the architectural structure of the unconscious.

By evoking set after set of derivatives of the unconscious, psychoanalysis increases the reach and depth of unconscious thinking, and thereby expands the unconscious mind itself.

Psychoanalysis and creativity

Free association is a form of personal creativity. Patients release themselves to speak the impressions of life, not knowing what sort of pattern of thought will emerge on any given day; each session will be unrepeatable and quite different from any other session. Often patients will be surprised by their patterns of thought and the logic of unconscious interests. Yet at the same time something will seem invariant, something about the self's idiom of being.

The Freudian Pair enables the analysand to feel the echo of his or her being in the method within which the analysand is a vital participant. It is like seeing one's soul in a particular type of mirror. Sessions vary, and one's unconscious interests are infinitely diverse, but one's way of composing oneself, one's others and one's world reveals a style that is forever individual and inseparable from one's identity.

Patients sense how psychoanalysis develops unconscious capabilities, enhancing the articulation of their idiom through the representational form peculiar to the Freudian Pair. Although this new form of creativity – in being and relating – is intangible and a part of immaterial reality, it can nevertheless be felt and is something of an acquired emotional talent.

Affect, emotion, feeling

We tend to use the words 'affect', 'emotion' and 'feeling' interchangeably, but it is useful, at least for psychoanalytical purposes, to distinguish between them.

Affects are phenomena such as anxiety, rage and euphoria, in their pure, essential form. They are part of the raw material of our internal life.

An emotion is a complex phenomenon that forms a new unit of self experience. It includes affect, but it is also a condensation of many other elements, such as ideas, memories, unconscious perceptions, derivatives of somatic states, and other mental ingredients. Emotions may become conscious, or they may remain entirely unconscious.

The English word 'emotion' derives from the Latin *movere*, 'to move'. When we say we are 'moved' by something, this indicates emotion's sequential, evolving aspect. (Affects, in themselves, do not include this element of movement.) Whilst we can assume that many members of the animal kingdom experience some form of affect, emotions can be experienced only by humans and some higher forms of animal life, as they involve the ability to link affects with ideas and an awareness of memories.

To describe the perception of affect or emotion we commonly use the word 'feeling'. This has connotations of a physical sense – that of touch. Feeling, when used to refer to the psychic rather than the somatic, can in fact be considered as a separate sense. Just as our eyes see the visual world, we feel the emotional world: we sense emotional states in ourselves and others. The capacity to use this sense of feeling will vary according to the degree of development of an individual's emotional life – which, in turn, will grow out of the quality of our experiences in infancy, which form a sort of unconscious emotional data bank.

A feeling, then, is a form of unconscious perception based on the matrix of emotional life. Empathy, in turn, derives from feeling emotional qualities in the other.

Patient and analyst share both ideas and emotions interwoven in the matrix of the Freudian Pair's creation of its own meshwork. This constitutes the unconscious field in which analysis takes place, and much of the time both participants are guided by their evolving emotional states. Such states of mind are actually complex unconscious organisations of those issues preoccupying the patient which, when articulated through the medium of the analytical method, bring about emotional organisations in each participant. Why is the analyst moved by a particular image? Why does he or she choose to repeat one specific word and not another? Often it will be because the analyst feels it is important, without knowing why.

If one's emotional life is well developed then one has the capacity to feel the impressions of life. Empathy – the capacity to put oneself into the other's position – is a developed ability: one learns how to feel one's way into the other. Free association and evenly suspended attentiveness permit the analyst a heightened ability to sense the patient, with this ability to feel deriving from the cumulative educational effect of emotional experience.

We can see how a condensation of ideas – an important part of Freud's theory of the unconscious – also becomes a dense affective experience, as the various different affects evoked by the separate ideas are brought into relationship. When ideas are gathered into a unity, such as a dream, the unravelling of this compaction through free association will often therefore involve an emotional experience – a 'moving experience' which derives from the lived structure of emotional organisation.

All people experience affects – and it is hard to imagine a human being who would not have at least something of an emotional life. But some people, notably those termed 'alexithymics', are so defended against affects that their emotional life is extremely restricted: they have an impoverished ability to feel. Psychoanalysis develops this capacity to feel, which is, in turn, an important feature of the capacity to intuit. Intuition is feeling-intelligence: the skill an individual has in discerning something about the other through what nowadays is also termed 'emotional literacy'.

If one of the aims of a psychoanalysis is to make the unconscious conscious, then another objective – or a wonderfully unwitting benefit – is to develop unconscious capabilities, thereby (amongst other effects) developing intuition.

Painters, novelists, composers and others in the 'creative arts' have long been interested in Freud's method, especially free association. Freudian ideas have certainly influenced the surrealist device of contiguous disconnected images that link in some unconscious manner; and the 'stream of consciousness' novel also plays upon the meaning of sequential thought. It is likely, however, that these formal adoptions of aspects of the psychoanalytic method are metaphors of a more profound sense of affinity with psychoanalysis as creative form. It is not so much that writers, painters and musicians consciously use the Freudian method in their work; it is more that they recognise psychoanalysis as a kindred form of creativity.

The ways in which psychoanalysis develops the mind itself, the ways in which it becomes a new form of creativity in living, and its after-effects on the subsequent life of the analysand: all are still to be properly recognised and understood.

Mother dream and father thought

Freud credited his patients with helping him to discover the free associative method. Free association took over where forced hypnosis had governed, when one of his patients apparently asked him to be quiet one day, so that she could just talk.

We cannot bid goodbye to this topic without considering what the psychoanalytical method of free association accomplishes simply by operating. Encouraged to bring a dream to the session for its reporting, the patient feels supported in bringing something from the infantile relation – for sleep is a return to foetal postures and to the hallucinatory thought of the infant – into the light of day. Some psychoanalysts think of the dream as a trace of the mother's body, so to some extent the analyst encourages the patient to bring his or her relation to the mother into the analytical space. Once there, the patient is obliged to report the dream.

In a sense, therefore, a facet of the father's law – described by Lacan as all obligations determined by one's place in the patriarchal hierarchy – is at work. However, the requirement is remarkably laid-back: simply say what is on the mind in association to the dream. The analyst does not interrogate the patient or demand that the patient make sense of the dream. Instead the patient lingers with the dream text, borrowing from its form, and talking without knowing much of what this means, rather like the dreamer inside his or her own dream. But as time passes and the analysand follows different lines of thought, the unity of the dream seems to break down and the associations take the dreamer very far away from the dream experience. Indeed, this process seems to be a kind of voyage towards many co-existing meanings, some of which are becoming clear to the patient. The dream as an event that might have seemed self-explanatory is now a dim memory. That oracular aspect of the dream – the maternal oracle that held the dreamer inside it, spoke in the dreamer's ear, brought visionary events before the dreamer's very eyes – is displaced by the dreamer's own mental life.

In this ordinary but remarkable way, psychoanalysis unites each analysand with the maternal world, yet marries that world with the paternal order; the patient is asked to keep the process of communication going even as he or she is aware of drifting away from the dream. Psychoanalysis thus reunites the patient with the mother, yet integrates the law of the father into the rendezvous, and separates the analysand from the belief that mother knows it all.

There is a widespread contempt for unconscious life in modern culture, in striking contrast to the general interest in associations, word plays and unconscious events in Freud's time. Attacks on psychoanalysis are thinly disguised attacks on unconscious life itself. One of the remarkable accomplishments of the Freudian Pair is both to facilitate the return of the analysand to the dream (and to maternal origins), and to foster a process of separation and individuation authenticated entirely by the patient's own associations. What separates the patient from the wish to remain inside the maternal oracle, or to be dependent on the analyst–father's interpretive truths, is the logic of the analysand's free associations. Over time these associations instantiate the patient's own idiom of thinking, and provide the basis upon which the patient can appreciate the value of the self's unconscious creativity.

2

Architecture and the unconscious

In interesting ways the world of architecture – broadly defined here as the deliberate consideration of the constructed human environment – and the world of psychoanalysis – broadly stated, the place for the study of unconscious mental life – intersect. A building derives from the human imagination, in some dialectic that is widely influenced by many contributing factors: its stated function, its relation to its neighbourhood, its functional possibilities, its artistic or design statement, its client's wishes, the anticipated public response, and many other factors that constitute its psychic structure. Even if the building springs from the known idiom of its architect and is clearly a Le Corbusier or a Mies van der Rohe, it will still have passed through many imaginings, influenced by many factors, the totality of which will be part of the architect's unconscious direction of the project.

We know that there is an unconscious life to each self. Is there an architectural unconscious, that is, a type of thinking which directs the projection of a building, influenced by many demands, yet finding its own vision out of the constituent elements?

Interestingly, Freud attempted to use the image of a city as a metaphor of the unconscious. In *Civilisation and its Discontents*, maintaining that 'in mental life nothing which has once been formed can perish', he reckoned that if we wished to imagine the unconscious we could do so by visualising Rome in such a way as to see all its periods – the *Roma Quadrata*, the *Septimontium*, the Servian Wall period, and the many Romes of the emperors to follow – at the same time. 'Where the Coliseum now stands,' he wrote, 'we could at the same time admire Nero's vanished Golden House.'[25]

Freud abandoned his metaphor because, as buildings are demolished and replaced in the course of time, a city is not a suitable example for the timeless preservations of the unconscious. Perhaps if Freud had sustained the metaphor a bit longer its dialectic would have worked. For obliterations are indeed part of one's unconscious life – so much so that depending on how one wished to look at the Rome of one's unconscious life, one could see both the preserved and the destroyed.

Certainly for architects and the cities or clients who employ them, destruction and creation bear an intimate proximity to one another. In the inner city most new builds are developed after the demolition of the former structure, one body standing where once another stood. For those who live through these moments there will always be two buildings in mind: the obliterated and the existent.

Ghost towns

I grew up in the small coastal town of Laguna Beach, some 45 miles south of Los Angeles. Even though it has had a surprisingly coherent and vigilant building code, which makes it difficult to build new structures, over time, of course, buildings have come and gone. At some point in the late 1950s an entire row of timber-framed buildings, fronting the main beach in the centre of town, was torn down – now revealing the sand and the sea to motorists passing along Highway 101. Whenever I think about it I can easily visualise these rather quaint seaside shanties, which housed such noteworthy occupants as a photographer's studio, a café, a chemist, a typical beachwear store, an orange juice stand, and the like. I visit the town several times a year and when my friends and I meet, in the course of giving directions to one another, we often refer to places that no longer exist.

Each city has its ghost towns.

Although the ghosts will be the inhabitants whom one recalls (and here I think of our town's first educated book dealer, Jim Dilley, and his glorious bookshop, now long since gone), the presence of the ghosts is, of course, entirely a matter of one's own unconscious life. I know of these places because I visited them. I loved the hamburgers in Bensons; I recall the stools at the counter where one sat, and the handsome machinery lining the wall, like the malt makers. So the energy of the ghost is of course my own: the ghost as the occupant who has suffered a trauma and is not yet prepared to leave this world is of course me. I have suffered the shock of losing this favoured place, and until I die it shall always be somewhere in mind.

To lesser and greater extent, this is true of all of us, especially when we move house. To leave a home, even when the contents go with us, is to lose the nooks and crannies of parts of ourselves, nesting places for our imagination. Our belief in ghosts will always be at least unconsciously authorised by the fact that we shall always linger on in our former houses, just as we assume that upon moving into a new dwelling, its former inhabitants will also still be there.

Architects mess with this psychic reality. Usually the ruthlessness of demolition is allowed its curiously stark nobility. A bulldozer (or its equivalent) arrives, we watch the structure dispatched in a surprisingly short period of time, and the earth – at least for a moment – receives sunlight once again. Sometimes architects will honour the demolished, as Evans and Shalev did in the Tate Gallery at St Ives in Cornwall. The new gallery was built on a site occupied by a gas tower; even though it was rather unsightly during its day, it was still the former occupant, and is now remembered in the rounded shape of the museum which mirrors it.

The wreckers

Who drives the wreckers?

Like the dreaded visits of the grim reaper in the literary imagination, the wreckers seem to be death on our doorsteps. Their actions are irreversible. Once they take out a building, it is gone for ever. So when notice is given to a community that a sector will be destroyed and something new will be built, even if the project is promising, there is always a certain dread of witnessing the efficiency of these wreckers. Of course, it is also exciting: like watching a fire or a flood wipe out an object, the sight of the wreckers brings out something of the child in us who builds sand-castles and delights in destroying them. On this side of the psychic equation is liberation from our attachments, and just as the child takes pleasure in destroying his or her creations – part of signifying the growing pleasure of leaving the secure architecture of the world created by mother and father to strike out alone – the adult watching demolition has his or her attachments wrested away.

Demolition is sacrificial. Before too long we shall be eradicated from this earth of ours, removed gracelessly from our spaces, our place to be taken by the other. Until that day, removals will seem like sacrificial offerings: at least I do not go with the obliterated. Well, not entirely. A part of me goes, a part I can apparently live without. Destruction of a building I like is emotionally painful, but I carry with me certain memories of the structure.

The work of the architect, then, involves important symbolic issues of life and death. Demolishing the existent structure to make way for a new one plays upon our own sense of limited existence and foretells our ending. Given this psychic issue, buildings seem to opt for one of two possible alternatives.

In one option they may either blend fully into their surroundings, as if to deny that a new build is anything new at all, or differ slightly from their fellow structures, as the seemingly logical extension of a seamless progression in architectural time.

Signs of the future

The second option is a radical departure from past and present: to declare themselves in the human future. If taking the latter solution – we may think of Richard Rogers' and Renzo Piano's Beaubourg, or Frank Gehry's Bilbao – these structures may seem more than simply buildings, rather material testimonies to our vision of the future. As such, we might identify with them. As they shall outlive us, they shall nonetheless signify us in the future, giving us a place in historical time and the existential reality of future generations who, upon gazing at these objects, may think of our era.

However, to identify with a building as a testimony of our intelligence cast into the future, it must be both beyond our immediate vision and yet not so far into the future as to alienate the imaginative idiom of our generation. If a building goes too far into the future – as the Eiffel Tower may have done in its day – the people feel a reverse effect: the future has invaded the present and cast scorn on that present's sensibilities.

Building is a form of prayer. Through our structures we pray that our minds and hearts have been well guided and that time will prove those structures to be true. Yet the very mass of a building – going back to the ziggurats of the Sumerians, the pyramids of Egypt, the temples of Greece – incorporates the tension of the living and their death. Such noble structures are, one way or the other, intended to honour the gods who live in eternity, and are offerings of our own limited being to the limitless. Buildings are, therefore, always verging on the profane: how dare we build anything for the gods?

Dead labour

The monumental structure – the mountain built by men – is one of the great paradoxes of architectural accomplishment. The monument is meant to outlive generations of men; yet in its construction many lives will be lost. Some, like Gaudí, who work their entire lives on the monument, will never see its completion.

All monuments, whether functionally intended so or not, are tombs. They not only shadow the deaths of the workers, and outlive their creators; they seem in their mass to be forms of death amongst the living.

Is architecture invested, then, with the grave task of bringing death into human life? Are these monuments houses of death? Does the immense implacability of the mass signify the destruction of the organic in the hands of the inorganic?

If so, then monumental structures are highly ambiguous objects. Out of the materials of the earth, we create a symbol of our death, sometimes as a tomb proper – as with the pyramids – but most often as a functional object presumed for the living, such as a great temple, cathedral or office building. If meant for the living, the monument is a kind of play-space within a death zone, as the living animate the cold marble or mass of cement, day after day during their lifetimes, before dying as new generations walk in the same space. Monuments allow us to move into and out of death space, the human being travelling in the world of great stone mass.

Like the sepulchre, however, we aim to put some sign of our lives on the monument, either in the form of ornament – aimed to be a sign of life inscribed into the death object – or, as in Greek nomenclature, by giving the parts of the building human names, such as the head of a column, or the throat of a chimney. As an embodiment of the real – understood here as the material expression of death that eludes our ultimate knowing – does the monument allow our signatures? Does it express human frivolity? Does the architect's imagination slightly mock its towering mass, such as Philip Johnson's AT&T (Sony) Building in New York? Or, as with Stalin's proposed Palace of the Soviets and Mussolini's architecture, does it show no sign of irony, no human dimension revealed in its massiveness?

Monuments and vivid built structures are evocative objects. 'A distinctive and legible environment not only offers security but also heightens the potential depth and intensity of human experience,' writes Kevin Lynch.[26] Objects possess degrees of 'imageability', he maintains, and certain cities have a higher degree of imageability than others. If monuments are forms of death in life, then they play both sides of the struggle between life and death, as they are also perceived as places of safety. During differing eras of the Egyptian dynasties the people took refuge in the walled-in temple cities and may well have joined those merchants and persons of standing who occupied dwellings next to the sacred place. Perhaps, like a chap called Panemerit, they built their house 'in the first temple courtyard up against the pylon, so that his statues should derive virtue from the sacred rites'.[27]

Panemerit may have believed he was holier because he lived close to a sacred place; perhaps he hoped that the journey after his death would be a favourable one. Whatever this meant to him, it was inescapably an emotional experience, perhaps layered by many different intersecting meanings. Those who live near La Scala, the Empire State Building or the Golden Gate Bridge experience what Minkowski called the 'reverberation' of the object. As particular objects are constructed and we dwell upon them, 'we ask ourselves how that form comes alive and fills with life . . . we discover a new dynamic and vital category, a new property of the universe: reverberation.'[28] La Scala might be the spirit of great operatic music, the Empire State of corporate virility, the Golden Gate of bridging the waters.

Some anthropologists believe that the ziggurats were either memories of mountains, left behind by the Sumerians who migrated from a more mountainous northern region to the Tigris–Euphrates delta, or simply devotions to the mountain as a noble object of nature.[29] Hersey believes that Greek temples may well derive from sacred trees. He points out how many differing human and environmental objects are given place in Greek buildings, through inclusion by name.[30] Lynch argues that vivid landscapes are 'the skeleton upon which many primitive races erect their socially important myths'[31], incorporating the striking objects of the environment into their cultural visions. Bachelard muses that through reverberation 'we feel a poetic power rising naively within us. After the original reverberation, we are able to experience resonances, sentimental repercussions, reminders of our past.'[32]

Our worlds

Great mountains, large rivers, the sea, the prairie, the jungle and remarkable edifices are etched in our mind like psychic structures; each seems to possess its own small universe of emotion and meaning. Every Venetian school-child learns to draw a map of how to get from home to school, as Venice is a city where one can easily become lost. These children's maps show how striking buildings are important markers for one's basic sense of orientation. St Mark's Square, for some, would be a lifelong sign of the orienting function of the object world that is essential to human survival, not unlike the sight of the beacon from the lighthouse during a fog, or the enduring presence of the national parliament during a time of war, and so on.

In his remarkable work *The Poetics of Space*, Gaston Bachelard calls for a 'topoanalysis' which would be 'the systematic psychological study of the sites of our intimate lives'[33]. There is, for example, a 'transsubjectivity of the image' so that those of us situated next to prominent sites share the image – even though, of course, each of us renders it differently. Lynch has found in his comparative analysis of Boston, Jersey City and Los Angeles how important it is to the citizens to have legible objects with high imageability. People in Boston, for example, contrasted buildings based on their age difference, while people in Los Angeles were of the impression that 'the fluidity of the environment and the absence of physical elements which anchor the past are exciting and disturbing'[34]. Inhabitants of Jersey City, a colourless industrial city close to New York, suffered from 'the evident low imageability of this environment' as they found it difficult to describe differing parts of their city, felt a general dissatisfaction living there, and were poorly oriented.[35] Living in a city, then, is to occupy a mentality. To be in Los Angeles is quite different from being in Boston.

How would a topoanalysis deconstruct the mentality of a city? We could hardly argue that a city reflects a singular unified vision. We know that there are many competing interests and diverse perspectives that generate differing structures. What would drive such a mentality? What would sustain it?

Winnicott argued that each mother provides her infant with an environment. In the beginning it is a 'holding environment', as one is literally embraced and moved about by the mother's self and her deputised objects (a walker, a toy car or a cot, for example). This holding environment sustains something of our earliest senses of being held, as we spend our first nine months as occupants of the womb. In his essay 'Berlin Walls', Winnicott considers the wider concept of environmental provision and its effect upon the development of people: 'The inherited maturational processes in the individual are potential and need for their realisation a facilitating environment of a certain kind and degree.'[36] Boston, Los Angeles and Jersey City are facilitating environments as they direct their occupants in differing ways. One of the mother's tasks, argued Winnicott, was to present objects to her infant. This was something of an art, for if she forced a new object upon the infant, the child would inevitably turn away; but if she allowed for 'a period of hesitation' during which the infant would turn away, presumably from lack of interest, the infant would soon enough return with heightened interest and desire towards the new object. In this respect, cities continually present their inhabitants with new objects – and the planning stage, when proposals are floated in the press, may constitute an important psychic element in the population's relation to the new.

Numerous plans for celebrating the turn of the millennium were floated in the UK, evoking almost universal opposition. In part it was because any supposed public spending on what seemed a frivolous adventure was objectionable. The eventual choice of site – an unpleasant post-industrial area of Greenwich Peninsula – was like foregrounding the Jersey City of London in the mind's eye of Londoners. Time needed to pass before the very idea itself could become acceptable. It is more than interesting that the gigantic object which the British selected for the centrepiece of the Millennium Dome was, initially, to be the body of a woman next to her child, so that queues of visitors would experience a showcase of Britain by climbing into a woman. It was finally decided to create two anodyne figures, a desexualisation of the bodies which still indicated one was entering two human forms: one big, the other small.

Unlike the Statue of Liberty, into whom one could climb (until its closure following September 11, at least) in order to see if one could get to the top – a rather phallic object, suggesting an equally phallic conclusion to inner exploration – the Dome woman was to have reclined, hands extended behind her, while the population entered just about where the womb would be, to gaze at exhibits of the internal organs of the body.

The living city

The Millennium Dome structure, again a Richard Rogers project, was however simply another expression of the British mentality, realised through the work of architecture. Taking Winnicott's view that a holding environment is an act of psychic intelligence, then a city is a living form that holds its population. Mentality is the idiom of holding, reflecting the very particular culture of place. No vision of it becomes its totality; in those epochs when men have attempted to impose a totalitarian vision of a city, it has denuded its population. Part of the error of such thinking, it seems to me, is the view that consciousness alone can form a city. Cities are rather unconscious processes. There are so many competing functions, aesthetics, local interests and economics, with each element influencing the other, that a city is more like the seeming chaos of the unconscious mind. Indeed it bears rather striking similarity to any ordinary self which has biological, sexual, historical, spiritual, vocational, familial and economic interests, all of which find themselves interlaced in some kind of moving form that gives rise to a type of organising vision, or mentality. Psychoanalysts working with a person long enough enter into a very particular culture, not unlike moving into a city and coming to know its oddities: its aesthetic preferences, its dislikes, its overcome obstacles, its wastelands, its partitioning of interests and its long-standing conflicts.

When evocative structures are built they will give rise to intense associations in the population. For example, when the Getty Museum in Los Angeles opened it was the object of widespread critical response. Driving north on Interstate 405 towards West Los Angeles, one sees on the hillside an evocative cultural object, 'speaking' to us through our associations. Before its opening the Getty was just a new rather impressive building; but now it is part of what it means to be Los Angeles. These elaborations, however, will eventually subside, and like the Metropolitan Museum of Art in New York or any other imposing museum, such disruptive impacts on the inhabitants of its time will be lost on future generations, who will subject it to their own sensibilities. Indeed, as we walk or drive through our cities, we know relatively little – if anything at all – about the great majority of structures. Once evocative, at least to the locals affected by their arrival, they are now like silent obelisks which would require considerable historical work and decoding to resurrect their voices.

So we are back to death yet again. Our cities contain hundreds and thousands of buildings which, once alive as evocative objects and part of the culture of place, are now cemeterial. In our consideration of the unconscious life of a city, then, we must reckon with a certain mute presence, a silenced voice, that perhaps is evidence in the everyday of the dying of the voice of the built. We know, don't we, that even simple buildings have stories to them. These tombs of the unknown citizens are nonetheless a part of our life and of living in the quotidian. The silence of the buildings is a premonitory presence of our own ending, inevitably part of our life. We could, if we so wished, put placards on each building, giving the date of completion, the name of the architect, a list of the workers, and perhaps selected local response from newspapers or oral notations. For the most part, however, we choose not to do this. Even the architects who build great structures are usually forgotten, unless, like Eiffel, their name – for better or worse – is identified with the object.

Remembering a name is a curiously conflicted event. Most people like wandering in a wood or gazing at wildflowers, but how many people can identify more than ten trees? We eat a fair amount of fish, but how many know what a cod, a turbot or a monkfish look like? Freud's theory of repression suggests that if we know the name of an object it generates a greater network of personal meaning, as names distinguish objects and interact rather intelligently with other names, in the moving psychic experiences of everyday life. The word 'oak', for example, designates a unique tree, but it also contains the phoneme 'oh' within it, and it could suggest 'yoke' and its meanings. If we knew all the names of the different trees in the forest, then as we saw a birch, a laurel, a dogwood, a maple, or the endless other trees, we would also be in a symphony of phonemes that would be playing along with the visual order. If we knew the names of our buildings, the years in which they were completed, and the names of their architects, we would also create a wider and denser universe of personal meaning.

Why don't we do this?

Nameless forms

The problem cannot simply be intellectual or cognitive. We have much less difficulty learning a foreign language or the characters of novels than we do remembering the names of trees, plants or fish – yet these objects are more immediately a part of our everyday life than Emma Bovary or the French for 'Please direct me to the nearest tourist office.'

At first glance it would seem as if we have a certain lack of interest in trees, plants, fish or our buildings. Are they of so little interest to us? It would seem this is hardly the case. So why are we mute when it comes to naming these visual objects? Perhaps the answer lies in the unconscious meaning of beholding a form which we treasure. Imagine for a moment that we do indeed like trees, that flowers and plants are very important, and that certain built structures, about which we know nothing, are truly important to us. They are part of our visual life. Perhaps they are intended to remain in that order of perception and imagination, fundamentally as silent visual objects.

I remember driving across the Plains states in North America, where to this day one may travel for hours without ever seeing another car. Countless American novelists and poets have likened the tall grass to a vast sea, as it moves in the breeze like ocean waves on a flat plane unmodified by hills. The sky and the prairie seem to meet in one continuous vast canvas. Now and then you will see a tree. As they can be miles apart, a single tree stands out in all its formal beauty as the essence of tree. A farmhouse, separated visually from any other farmhouses, can be seen for miles, and as you approach it, it seems to embody the essence of a house. A flash of lightning in the distance, a cloud passing across the sky, a flock of birds, a field of sunflowers, a tractor: all of these objects stand out in stark singularity against the silence of the background. Each object seems to be the spirit of its brothers, one tree standing for the existence of all trees, one house standing for the presence of all houses. It is as if one contemplates the purity of a form.

Perhaps we choose to ignore the naming of objects because we find ourselves more moved by their form. Until we know the precise name we know only its generic name, and this may be a compromise between the natural world and the built environment. Perhaps we choose to walk only amongst the trees, the plants or our streets, in order to commune with form itself. When we break down these forms and give them their names, whose names do we use? Do the names derive from the form itself? Of course not. The names derive from that patriarchal order which arbitrarily names objects. So to defy the knowing of the names may well be to decline the secularisation of objects which we believe carry great spiritual weight.

Buildings and structures that become nameless, that simply meld into the matrix of a city, may fulfil our need for nameless forms, rather like pure objects unsullied by knowledge. We choose to live in the visual, not the verbal, order. We choose, therefore, to live part of our life in the maternal order – that register of perception guided by the maternal imaginary – rather than in the paternal order, which names objects and possesses them in language. And part of our wandering in this visual world – that shall go nameless – is to meander, then, in the preverbal world: one organised around sights, sounds, smells and affinities. This is a world of ours that has in many respects gone by. One's life within one's mother and then alongside her, before one knows about obligations and speech, fades and fades with age. Like the silent buildings with no name, the maternal order is rather lost upon the workaday maturity of the languaged self.

If we need to know the names of streets, and the names and locations of many different public buildings – from the motor vehicle licensing office to the opera house, from the tax office to the post office, from the ticket office to the best bookshop – we may also need to walk among many buildings that shall be without name.

Our paths

'Every citizen has had long associations with some part of his city,' writes Lynch, 'and his image is soaked in memories and meanings.'[37] As we walk or travel about our city we select various routes, each of which has differing evocative effects. 'What a dynamic, handsome object is a path,' writes Bachelard[38] – as those paths we choose are lined by objects that shall play upon our mind. Even though certain routes will be ordained by the mentality of the city (so that in taking the highway to the airport, or the only road to the ferry, we are guided by the intelligences of form of those who have planned and executed the routes), we elect our own paths throughout our life. During a year lived in New York City, I had a wide choice of routes from my home on West 94th Street to my office on East 65th Street. I had to cross Central Park, which offers innumerable paths. Although I walked different ways when I tired of my favoured route, I enjoyed one particular path. I walked along Central Park West as far as 81st Street, which gave me a long vista of the west side and the families spilling out of the elegant apartment blocks on to the streets. I entered the park and walked between the Great Lawn and

Turtle Pond – the field the location of baseball pitches and the pond full of ducks and turtles. I then either walked through a tunnel and along the edge of the Metropolitan Museum of Art, or across a street to Cherry Hill, before winding my way from 72nd and Fifth until arriving at my destination.

Each segment of this journey is well known to me. Each unit has its own 'structural integrity', that is, its own particular character. But of course what they evoked in me will differ from what they evoke in another person. And although I enjoyed being lost in thought during this walk, I was certainly inspired by the sequential implications of each integral form. One is, as Blake's poem suggests, always a 'mental traveller' in this world, and the paths we choose to take in our lives – even as simple as the way I walked to work – are vital parts of the expression of our own personal idiom.

Each city, then, has its own structural integrity (the material realisation of imagined forms) through which we travel. Cities evolve their own interspatial relations as roads intersect, as parks are placed, as high streets are segregated from residential areas, as industrial parks are segregated from art centres, and so on. If spatialisation were the unconscious development of space according to the evolution of any city, then interspatial relations would define the psychology of spaces as they relate to one another, and as they invite the citizen to move across boundaries and into new 'nodes' that define areas. Moving in this unconscious organisation of sites and their functions is the individual, who will elect favoured paths and who will, quite idiosyncratically, find certain locations more evocative than others. Most obviously this occurs when one has been raised in a particular 'neck of the woods', so that the objects experienced during childhood will contain parts of the self's experience that will have been projected into the objects as mnemic containers of lived experience. But in time, any individual will find a new area more interesting in some respects and less interesting in others, as he or she gravitates towards certain objects that become points of personal reverie.

Walking and evocation

Walking between the Great Lawn and Turtle Pond, I am between two distinct structures (one a field of Kentucky Green Grass with baseball diamonds here and there, the other a large pond with a rock cliff on one side and a marsh-to-grass sector on the other) serving public visions (the field for human play, the pond for observation of natural life) but each structure evokes associations peculiar to my life.

To take the Great Lawn. As a structure in its own right, with its own integrity, there is a simple beauty about a baseball field. The diamond shape of the 'infield' is earth, while the 'outfield' is grass. In a well-groomed baseball field the contrast between the grass and the earth is beautiful. As a purely empty space – minimalist, as it excludes the players – it is like a familiar, though varied, rendition of a potential space. When the players occupy the field, usually in brilliantly different costumes, a baseball diamond is like a Paul Klee painting – especially if one considers the teams upon teams that shall occupy the space. Each team has nine participants who, though occupying set positions, will move out of place – creating lines of movement against the earth/green outline of the pitch – becoming a figurative form of abstract expressionism: the figures who move create the abstraction that gives the game its visual poetry.

The Great Lawn, considered not as an integral but as an evocative object – something that inspires idiosyncratic parts of myself which have been projected into that space during the course of my lifetime – holds that part of me which nearly went on to play professional baseball in my youth. Depending on my frame of mind, on any day the sight of the Great Lawn may inspire differing types of memory: actual recollection, a type of mood, a wish to play the game.

But on the other side of me is Turtle Pond, which, though of course an integral object – something with its own structural integrity not altered by human projection – is also an evocative object. It does not bring to mind myself in my youth, but in my early forties, when I lived for two years in the countryside of western Massachusetts.

Although it does evoke the spirit of the pond – and certain recollections of the ponds of western Massachusetts – it also evokes memories of my place of work, of my family's interests, and quite personal issues deriving from that time of my life.

Without thinking about it much, when we traverse a city – or walk in our district – we are engaged in a type of dreaming. Each gaze that falls upon an object of interest may yield a moment's reverie – when we think of something else, inspired by the point of emotional contact – and during our day we will have scores of such reveries, which Freud termed psychic intensities, and which he believed were the stimuli for the dream that night. But as a type of dreaming in their own right, the reveries wrought by evocative objects constitute an important feature of our psychic lives.

People who dislike the area where they live are in a sad state of disrepair, for they are denied the vital need for personal reverie. Each person needs to feed on evocative objects, so-called 'food for thought', which stimulate the self's psychic interests and elaborate the self's desire through engagement with the world of objects. Indeed, although such movement is too dense to be interpreted, each person senses something of his or her own unique idiom of being as he or she moves freely through space. We will not know what that idiom is, but will sense that we are moving according to our own realised intelligence of form, shaping our lives through our selection of objects.

My walk through Central Park is not available to a simple psychoanalytic (or any other) interpretation, but the movement of inspired musings is uplifting and is part of the feeling that life is for the living, and not just for recumbent thinking or vocational productivity.

This prospect is not lost on architects, who certainly know of the evocative potential of any of their buildings, even if the precise idiom of reverie derived from the citizens would of course be largely unknowable. And although new towns may be said to have planned obvious places for reverie – parks and the like – the evocativeness of objects cannot be charted into a psychic journey, even if the layout of Disneyland in California (with no directions, just the next realm of fantasy life) attempts to prove the exception.

We know, however, that vivid structures find their way into our dreams at night, and it is here – in the dreamworld – that the visions of the architect and the dreams of the citizen find curious communion.

To the dream

Just as Athenians must certainly have had the Parthenon in their dreams, we too take vivid structures into our dreams; the unconscious that operates in the material realm of the built, and the unconscious that organises each self, meet. Visionary architects intend their structures to suggest dreams to their dwellers, but I shall maintain that all along we know that vivid structures will enter our dreams and affect our dream life. Indeed we might say that just as perspective in fine art was achieved through the architectural effects of Renaissance architecture (the extraordinary influence of Brunelleschi), our dream life is influenced by the perspectives accomplished in the architectural imagination. I had best give an example. I shall report a dream of mine:

I am walking down a sloping street in Laguna Beach that leads to Victoria Beach. I am with my wife, my father and mother, my next youngest brother and my son, and we are all in a mood to hang out on the beach. I look to the right and, to my surprise, see the reflection of a wave breaking over a high cliff that is rimmed with tall trees. The wave is bright green and translucent so that it does not actually obliterate the sight of the cliff and the trees. Above the wave is a brilliant blue sky and the overall effect is visually astonishing. I point this out to my family and we are all amazed and delighted, and head toward the beach with even greater enthusiasm. Although the event is felt to be remarkable, it is not understood to be unusual. In the next scene we are bathing in the water, in really quite big waves. I see my father, with arms crossed, floating in the white water right up to the shore, being carried along and obviously enjoying himself. In the final scene I am leaving my family at our favourite outdoor restaurant near Main Beach (about two miles from Victoria Beach) in order to nip off to Dilley's Bookstore. The mood of the dream is one of well-being.

Certain facts shall help illuminate part of the dream, which I shall not subject to analytical association or interpretation, but shall instead use to illustrate a specific point. The dream took place approximately a year after my father's death; his ashes were scattered at sea off Laguna Beach. Victoria Beach was the place where we hung out as a family, until I was 14 years old. Up to about the age of ten, I was not permitted by my father to go out into the very large surf, but instead had to play in the white water, indeed, in much the way my father did in the dream.

In a former restaurant of the Surf and Sand Hotel (about halfway between Victoria Beach and Main Beach) there was a mirror on the ceiling. Sitting at a table with a view of the sea, you could also look up and see the waves moving across the ceiling, which was an unusual and pleasant visual effect. I think I incorporated this design innovation into my dream, in that I saw the reflected wave breaking on the hill. But the object and its design origin – a mirror – seems also to be a part of the dream, as my father mirrors the way I swam as a boy. Only now, however, he is gone – dispersed in the sea – and although I may be the titular head of the family (victorious in the Oedipal sense, as in the name of the beach) my son is also along for the trip to the sea, and so, in a way, my own ending too is in sight.

The restaurant in the dream no longer exists, and neither does Dilley's Bookstore, except in my dream, or in the world of literature. Going off to the bookstore that is no longer there may very well have been a premonition in the dream of the task of writing this essay, which, not incidentally, is now written down and part of a literature of sorts.

For some days after the dream I asked myself a question that had occurred following previous memorable dreams. What is the function of such vivid beauty? Why does the unconscious bother to construct such a setting?

Perhaps because truly profound dreams are meant to be memorable, to be commemorated for ever through a high degree of imageability. Perhaps we are meant to pass them along from one generation to the next. And perhaps the part of us that constructs the unforgettable dream – alongside those that are more pedestrian – comes from the same part of us that seeks to build unforgettable structures.

Is visionary architecture a dreaming?

Buildings: between life and death

Do we intend monumental structures to be dreamt upon and to extend themselves into our dreams and those of the generations to come? Yet if they signify death on earth, the immobile inert mass of silence, why should they be vivid? Would we not want death to be as marginal and as inconspicuous as possible, and for as long as possible? The uncanny compromise achieved by the monumental is that it is both a sign of life and a sign of death. As we sleep, we all go off into a darkness, perhaps never to return. To dream is to take a sample of lived experience with us, indeed to take our entire history with us into the darkness. If we survive to live another day, so much the better. But our dream objects, the furniture of life, may be the last articles we see before everything goes completely and irreversibly dark. A monument that bears death in its mass, supposed ironic triumph of the inorganic over the organic, of the creation over the creator, may transcend its terminability with evocative suggestiveness. It intends, in other words, to stimulate the imagination as we walk about in the shadows of death.

One city in particular seems to have grasped the strange ambiguity of the monumental as intercourse between life and death. When the sun sets and dark descends in the Nevada desert, the city of Las Vegas comes alive as an extraordinary illumination of human fancy, perhaps capitalising in all respects on the wishful nature of the dream event. By day the buildings of Las Vegas are simply rather dead and uninteresting, all the more reason for its visitors to sleep during the day (perhaps keeping the city of the night alive in the dream) waiting for the moment to wake up and re-enter the night vision. One lives in the midst of a type of managed dream in Las Vegas, which in the past two decades has broadened the scope of its dream furniture to include the cities of New York, Venice and Paris, and the Egyptian pyramids. Perhaps the world is dreaming itself through this architectural structure, as if the planners of Las Vegas, having astutely extended the evocative function of design to influence the dream life of citizens, have found a place where design and dream can meet in the middle of the night to the profit and loss of both participants.

Architects intermittently play with the idea of meeting the self's desire for the integral object's other function (that of evocation). On the slope of a hill leading from Hampstead Village to Golders Green in North London lies a well-known English progressive school. The buildings of the King Alfred School (KAS) surround a large and irregular, but slightly circular, somewhat uneven playing field. From the small single-storey structures to the immediate left as one enters the school, where the younger children reside, moving clockwise around the field, other structures house the children as they grow up. The Lower School has several new builds from the last few years which catch the eye of visiting prospective parents as signs of modernity and good funding. At 12 o'clock are wooden fortress-like structures for the more adventurous, at 1 o'clock tennis courts and the gymnasium, at 2 o'clock a rectangular building constructed in the 1980s, at 2.45 a kind of pagan space called Squirrel Hall, surrounding a gigantic chestnut tree where the older and more wizened adolescents hang out, and at 3 o'clock is the Blue Building.[39] It is a new build which rises above an old temporary building on stilts, so that one day when the school can afford to remove the old building, the stilts will act as the new skin of what would then be a new structure.

Prospective parents and school members view the spirit of progressive education in this structure, in part, because it signifies cost-saving inventiveness and integrative adaptation while at the same time coming across as quite innovative in its own right. The rectangular structure, the pagan area and the Blue Building bear little architectural integrity (as in most architectural evolutions, no plan would have intended this) but collectively they do seem to work in an odd kind of way. If we bear in mind that two tethered goats have the run of the large field in the centre and that the school's children and staff are all on first-name terms – and that children at different stages in their lives there construct small villages on the field to learn about materials, planning, execution and cohabitation – then the evolution of design at the King Alfred School seems to have captured the overdetermined capability of buildings.

The buildings are meant to serve functions, but they may also serve the differing evocative implications of their location. In the interesting rendezvous of children, parents, educators and administrators, buildings are constructed which reassure all (they can sleep in peace) and which constitute a kind of embodied dream.

A progressive school like KAS, even if endowed with the funds to do so, would not want to raze its existent structure and build an entirely new school. Nor would it want the temporary buildings (many now well into their thirtieth year) to exemplify too much the spirit that each child (in the form of each building) must be allowed to go forward at his own pace in respect of his or her progressive capacity. KAS is a kind of fairytale world for the diverse requirements of its participants, dreaming its way into shared reality at a pace that is just about right.

Set against these design dreams – of a Las Vegas or a KAS – are objects which would seem to be clearly meant to offend. Both the Eiffel Tower in Paris and the Post Office (BT) Tower in London were regarded as 'shit' by large proportions of the population when first constructed. What we might think of as archi-excretions – that is, buildings that seem intended to offend the population – are nonetheless interesting features of the architectural unconscious. The offensive object, or 'eyesore', may be created by the architect, or allowed to go into existence by the planners, as an unconscious defiance of the population: popular as notorious, putting noses up in the air out of offence. If we set aside simple sadism as the function of such offending acts, why might archi-excrement be tolerated?

The value of a mistake

Architecture, to develop, must make mistakes. As new materials develop they may outpace the architect's grasp of their limitations and for a while ugly structures will certainly be produced. But one generation's excremental object may be another generation's gold, as is somewhat the case with the Eiffel Tower these days: at least, so far as the visitors are concerned, who rather admire it.

The offensive object, however, may be unconsciously welcomed – even as it is consciously vilified – because it raises an interesting psycho-spiritual question. Is this self of ours, which is deposited upon this earth, nothing more than shit? As our bodies decay, as we see early signs of our wasting away, knowing that one day we shall be wormed to a kind of stinking waste, will anything come of this excretion? Will we ever truly be resurrected? How could anything be made out of our waste?

The same question is raised when architects create shit. Surely, the people wonder, how can this excrement ever come to anything? What form of intervention in the minds of the generations to come could possibly transform this dross to gold? Disguised in this offended frame of mind may well be a deeply hidden wish that, quite possibly, some day this building will be loved by those who surround it. Perhaps waste will be transformed into live matter. Perhaps the rejected will be the resurrected. But if so, this will happen in the minds of man. The eyesore, then, awaits a future frame of mind, perhaps one more sophisticated than our own, perhaps one that will function in the world of futuristic medicine, perhaps even in a world where, through DNA replication of our blood samples, we can be resurrected after all. Perhaps then, these piles of waste are strange prayers to the future, very different from those admired monuments discussed earlier.

New buildings, especially visionary ones, elicit the sounds of awe. In the visual field of the Empire State Building must be the auditory inscriptions of many an 'Ahhhh', 'Ooooh' or 'Wooow'. The mouth opens to take in the sight, the self perhaps thrown back to the infant's opened mouth of surprise as yet another astonishing new object is presented before it. Certainly the scale of New York puts all of us back into the realms of the child amongst the giants, but the spectacle of the object, its spectacular value, trades off the history of any self born into a world of surprises.

Equally the 'Yuuuck!' and the averted gaze express the unpleasures of the unwelcomed objects of one's beginnings. Alternatively the unspectacular, surprising design – for example, a newly built small shop that fits into a previously derelict sight rather nicely – might elicit an 'Ahhhh! I didn't know that was there.'

To build the evocative on whatever scale is to open the psyche-soma, seemingly expanding the mind and the body in one singular act of reception which links the new object to the pleasantly surprised subject. As discussed earlier, buildings trade on our unconscious awe of the stature of the physical world – the 'breathtaking' view of a mountain, the sea or the prairie – and to this extent they have an onto-logical potential: we may be returned to the origin of our being in its first perceptions of the object.

When this occurs the building occupies a certain spirit of place, its design establishing ontological value, as we are put back in the place of birth – as new objects open our mouths and our psyches to the continuing spirit of birth. If the body from whom we arrive, the mother, may be regarded as the god who delivers us into our being, then her subsequent presentation of objects may be seen as consecrations of the object world. Each object the infant puts into his or her mouth for the taste test is communion of the mother's breast.

In our unconscious, then, buildings sustain (or fail) this communion. This good breast, as Melanie Klein famously terms it, is disseminated in the object world, to be found for each person in those objects which either physically or psychically open the mouth and mind. New-found objects either pass or fail this taste test, and people will of course vary enormously in their idea of what is in good taste or in bad taste.

Is the sight divine or not?

Designers and architects, as we have seen, create a world of taste or for the taste, and inherit the task of the mother who delivers the self into a new place with new views and new objects. Cities will have well-known areas for the probably awe-inspiring; but the small material objects of life – a glass, cutlery, a lamp, etc. – are every bit as likely to carry this delight in them. Love of our objects, sometimes something of an embarrassment, is a passion that performs a communion.

Man-made

The man-made world contrasted with the natural world, however, raises a different duality, as built objects seem testimonies to the patriarchal order, while the natural world is likened to the maternal order. As discussed, however, there are countless forms of intercourse between the maternal and paternal orders. If we allow that the decision over insemination is a patriarchal action – take a Greek temple, for example – and its construction is named by man, then its birth to the newcomer (that is, the first moment of seeing it) always trades off maternal presentation of the surprising object. If the monument seems a hallmark of the monolithic triumph of the inorganic over our organic lives, then our giving its structure names from the parts of our bodies seeks inscription. These same temples also bear the names of parts of the animal and botanical world, just as cave paintings and Egyptian tombs bore representations or artefacts from the natural world.

We have been bringing together objects from the maternal order and the paternal order and from life forms and death forms since the beginning of time – a sequence of juxtapositions that is part of the unconscious obligation of architecture.

The park in the city, the garden at the back of the house, the potted plant in the room, the flowers in the vase:

these are emblems of the natural world in the built world, just as a small chapel in the forest or a sculpture in the meadow are signs of the built order in the natural world.

Spirits of place

These forms of intercourse are spiritual moments if we understand by this that each embodiment carries with it the spirit of the signifier. A flower in a vase is the spirit of flowers; a church in the woods is the spirit of Christian faith. City planning is not simply functional and locally meaningful: it also involves a type of psycho-spirituality, that is, it is invested with the psychological task of bringing the spirits of life into certain place.

As time does not permit what we might think of as a spiritual deconstruction of Western society – we could examine a house in terms of the spirit of its plumbing, or the spirit of its heating, or the spirit of its living space – let us limit ourselves to the spiritual representation of certain social phenomena vital to human life. We farm the land and we fish the seas. Our survival depends upon these two very ancient functions. In the modern city the fruits of farming and of fishing will of course find their way into the large supermarkets, but we might ask if architecturally we are succeeding in representing the spirit of the fisherman and of fishing as well as the spirit of the farmer and of farming.

Most cities do have open markets containing fishmongers and farm produce, and the market square bears something of these spirits. Fisherman or farmers, for example, visiting the market square will feel that their lives – and the world of fish or of crops – are represented to some extent. Yet sometimes city planners and architects do more than this. In Bergen, for example, in the central harbour there are several large fish tanks, so that citizens and tourists may gaze at these remarkable creatures from the other world moving about in tanks of seawater, well before they go elsewhere on their journey. The same presentation of the sea, its contents (the fish), and the lives of those men and women who work in this world (fishermen) are given honoured place in Helsinki and in Gothenburg. But a similar architectural representation of the spirit of fish disappeared quite some time ago from the area near the Old Town in Stockholm. We could call this a loss of one element of the city's spirit.

At the time of the Conservative Party's ruthless destruction of the mining communities of Great Britain, during Margaret Thatcher's era, Covent Garden (the former fruit and vegetable market of central London) was transformed into boutiques and tourist shops, with New Covent Garden Market having been previously re-sited many miles away. One need not quarrel with the structural necessity of these decisions: perhaps it was necessary to restructure the mining industry, just as it may have been to relocate and enlarge the produce market. But if my argument is correct, that planning and building is not simply functional, rather the work of meaning – indeed, the work of spiritual communion – then the eradication of such sites from the centre of a city amounts to a form of spiritual elimination.

One need only visit Pike Place in Seattle to see how the sea and the land can be functionally and spiritually located. Planning could easily allocate the vast majority of its fish, meat and agricultural processing to the perimeters of a city, while at the same time comprehending the need both of those who work in these distant fields and the people who live within the city to have a spiritual relation to one another. (Recall that by 'spirit' I mean the precise idiom of evocative effect derived from the integrity of each of these differing realms.)

There is no reason, then, why a city like London, for example, could not have in its centre a monument to the underworld of coal mining and to the spirit of mining. The great mining towns of Yorkshire and Wales could find spiritual representation in their capital city, were half a city block designed to reveal it. The same could go for the shipping industry, the automobile industry and so forth.

Such totems, as it were, would invite the spiritual worlds of man and woman into places of representation. However interesting and deeply meaningful monotheism has been, were the monotheistic drive to eliminate the spiritual world embodied in differing lesser gods (i.e. the corn spirit, the rain spirit, and so on), it would be a senseless eradication of the spirit of life on earth. We do all derive from the mother, and in that sense our monotheism is apt, but what kind of mother would we be recalling if honouring her was to be accomplished by destroying the embodied spirits of the object world that she set us into enjoying?

The monotheistic might then be a totalitarian spirituality presided over by what André Green terms the 'dead mother', a figure whose psychic anguish, self-preoccupation and dementia have precluded her passing her relation to her child on to the child's relation to reality.

The architectural unconscious

Part of the task of the architectural unconscious, then, may be to survive monotheistic genocide of difference and, through the diversity of structures, to at least provide the form for many spirits even if – as yet – the true houses for the spirits of life have yet to be fully comprehended and attended to.

Fifty years before the construction of the Eiffel Tower, Roland Barthes reminds us, the nineteenth-century novel materialised in the literary imagination that point of perspective creating a panoramic view that would be achieved in the technology of the Tower. In a chapter of *The Hunchback of Notre Dame* which gives a bird's-eye view of the city, and in Jules Michelet's *Tableau chronologique* which does the same, one looks out upon Paris, something one could do later following the Tower's construction. Barthes argues that travel literature had described scenes of life, but the traveller was always thrust into the midst of the scene, describing the sensation of the new; while from these novels and from the Tower 'a new perception' was born, 'that of concrete abstraction; this, moreover, is the meaning which we can give today to the word *structure*: a corpus of intelligent forms'[40]. Gazing down on Paris, one sees the structure of the city as a body of intelligent forms.

The multitude of co-terminus dialectics that drive the differing intelligences of a city – eradication and creation of new roads, new parks, schools, and so on – constitutes the body of a city's form. Like the unconscious life of any one self, the intelligence of a city's forming and transforming of itself derives from no single stimulus, but will always have been a dynamic matrix of many influences that nonetheless seems, in time, to create its mentality. Although that mentality, or let us say, collected vision – a dreaming derived from the many constituents – may be destroyed, once alive and in place it constitutes a very particular system unconscious that will generate the complex meanings of a city and its inhabitants.

Bion argued that mental life couldn't be assumed. The only reason we develop a mind, he maintained, is because we have thoughts and eventually thoughts demand the arrival of a thinker to think them. We have many experiences in life, but if these experiences are not transformed into some form of material for thought, then from Bion's point of view these would therefore be 'undigested experiences'. He gives the arbitrary sign B, or Beta, to such elements. But if the self's mind is forming then the ontic factors of life may find ontological significance, and we may derive food for thought, to which he assigns the term A or Alpha.

We may be able to borrow some of Bion's thinking to consider the life of a village or a city. The mere existence of buildings and cities does not mean that they have a mentality. They may once have been 'a corpus of intelligent forms', but now they could be dead. Those living in the city might be hard pressed to derive from the city's Beta functioning – that is, purely functional operation – any food for thought: it would not give rise to legends, myths, memories, dreams, contemplations or new visions, like Jersey City in the Lynch study. But if the city transforms itself, generating new forms of life, then it would be creating Alpha – that is, the food for thought – and the city's mentality, its unconscious forming of itself and its inhabitants, would be alive and well.

The topography of southern Orange County in California shows how so-called developers have tried to bypass the struggle to move from Beta to Alpha, from the undigested to the digested, through the creation of ready-made towns, with themes like 'Spanish Village', or 'Cape Cod'. Although the schools, parks, shopping malls and graded housing districts were executed in one single swift act of development, and certainly intending to exude the spirit of place (i.e. Spain or Cape Cod in California), cloning a mentality is not equivalent to working through those stages of human strife out of which a community grows its own true spirit.

The anodyne new towns of southern Orange County are the city equivalents of the human false self, an invented identity meaning to stand in for authentic civic life. These environments themselves suggest that their inhabitants share in a kind of shallowing out of the self, meant to live in apparent immediate normality, as if the theme-park city has true integrity. Such places would then be empty forms, falsely presumed intelligences, aiming to produce a mentality by copying and pasting other sites and mentalities to the new site. At the end of the day, a Lynch studying these cities would find, I think, that its inhabitants were possessed of a curiously dislocating contentedness: they have everything, and yet it would appear to mean nothing.

The study of unconscious life is a project that we associate with Freud's announcement of the formation of psychoanalysis. Still very much in its early stages as an intellectual project, Freud's designation should not stop with the limits of the individual self. Winnicott wrote:

A diagram of the human individual is something that can be made and the superimposition of a thousand million of these diagrams represent the sum total of the contribution of the individuals that compose the world and at the same time it is a sociological diagram of the world.[41]

It remains for us to follow the psychoanalytic project towards all its implications, not simply as has happened in the study of literature and culture, but elsewhere, as in the continued study of the unconscious dimensions of architecture, or what the French Situationist Guy Debord termed 'psycho-geography': 'the study and manipulation of environments to create new ambiences and new psychic possibilities'.[42]

3

The evocative object world

We have discussed how through free association we travel along trains of thought linked to the experiences of our daytime. The object world – its 'thing-ness' – is crucial to our use of it. As we move about, we live in an evocative object world that is only so because objects have an integrity of their own.

This integrity of an object – the character of its thing-ness – has an evocative processional potential. Upon use by the self, it may – or may not – put the individual through a complex psychosomatic experience.

All the time, as we amble about in our worlds, we come across objects, whether natural or man-made, material or mental. For the unconscious there is no difference between a material and a non-material evocative object; both are equally capable of putting the self through a complex inner experience. Wordsworth's memory of Grasmere was an internal mental phenomenon and the image of it in his mind was almost certainly more emotionally compelling than the actual sight of it. The adage that 'absence makes the heart grow fonder' may help us to see how a mental object, by virtue of the power of absence, crystallises memory so that mere mental recollection is redolent with meaning. The psychoanalytic observation that the absent mother is the more powerful inner presence for the infant – who is actively creating the mother in order to retain an object relation to her – testifies to the force of the internal evocative object.

Sometimes when people think of actual (i.e. external) things as evocative objects they become nostalgic. I am no exception – I have discussed the effect on me of the sight of a pond, or a baseball pitch, or other objects that evoke memories embedded in an object. These objects are often so important precisely because they are no longer present: we may be a long way from home. Nostalgia is the emotion of love lost, grief sustained and gratitude for the evocative power of memory that allows us to hold on to the lost object.

But the nostalgic object is only one amongst many possible forms of evocative object.

To visit any large department store, where one goes through the various sections – homeware, children's clothes, televisions, furniture – is to enter different categories of the evocative. Each section elicits within us a different psychic state. I love the kitchen sections. Even when I do not need to buy anything, I enjoy the sight and feel of the hefty food processors, or the frivolous popcorn makers. I can also spend time in front of those tableaux of small utensils – corn strippers, garlic mashers, wine stoppers – that are now almost fashion items. I hate the perfumery section and wonder why department stores have to locate these at the front entrance, forcing me to brave their olfactory assault.

Each section of the store, each part of the section, each unit of visual space, contains evocative objects. As we see them their design elicits feelings within us, their function comes to mind, their names – generic and brand – come up in consciousness. As to the unconscious registration of such objects, we can only assume that just as the store clusters like-objects in such units, our mind does much the same thing, with the salient exception that we add personal meaning to each and every one of the things we see.

But we do not just see them. We experience them.

Associating with objects

When we meander in the world of things, we may be doing so as free associating beings – governed by an underlying sequence in what seems to be random movement – but we will also be caught up in what we might think of as *islands* of emotional experience.

In the toy department, the sight of a particular model train might arrest me in time and space for a while, as the object launches a daydream. Such a daydream could take me back to my childhood. It could take me forward to imagining a moment when I might give it to a kid as a present. It could make me fear I will be stupid enough to buy it, and I might dream the look on my wife's face when I emerge from this section of the store: 'Oh, and what's in the package?'

The great American philosopher John Dewey wrote more on the nature of experience than any other writer of his time. Some of Dewey's comments bear strikingly on our discussion:

> Emotions are attached to events and objects in their movement. They are not, save in pathological instances, private. And even an 'objectless' emotion demands something beyond itself to which to attach itself, and thus it soon generates a delusion in lack of something real.[43]

In 'Having an Experience', published in 1934, Dewey argued that lived experience is not a continuous flow of mental and emotional life, but is divisible into units:

> We have *an* experience when the material experienced runs its course to fulfillment. Then and only then is it integrated within and demarcated in the general stream of experience from other experiences.[44]

Experiences have a beginning, a middle and an end. We can think of specific entities as units of experience. Dewey writes:

> An experience has a unity that gives it its name, *that* meal, that storm, that rupture of friendship. The existence of this unity is constituted by a single *quality* that pervades the entire experience in spite of the variation of its constituent parts.[45]

Dewey even comes up with his own take on free association, one that is strikingly similar to Freud's view:

Thinking goes on in trains of ideas, but the ideas form a train only because these are much more than what an analytic psychology calls ideas. They are phases, emotionally and practically distinguished, of a developing underlying quality; they are its moving variations, not separate and independent like Locke's and Hume's so-called ideas and impressions, but are subtle shadings of a pervading and developing hue.[46]

Like Freud, Dewey argues that we think along a sequential line – and he uses Freud's metaphor of the train of thought. Dewey believes that this flow of thought is demarcated by what we would now say are the boundaries of an emotional experience within the flow.

In *The Interpretation of Dreams* Freud argued that the unconscious is partly organised according to 'clusters of ideas'. The unconscious is a matrix that does clearly observe *differences* between areas of meaning.

Objects for thought

I think we may view Dewey's project as directed more toward the clusters of association that emanate from differing types of evocative objects. We have discussed the nostalgic evocative object that clearly does have an original temporal and spatial place in one's lifetime. It also comes with that 'hue' which Dewey described, or which Freud would term a 'high psychical value', or which contemporary philosophers would term 'qualia'.

In *The Freudian Moment*, in the chapter titled 'Psychic Transformations', I discussed some of the differing forms of thinking.[47] Transference is a form of thinking through enactment. Another way of thinking is via our engagement with actual objects in the world, through the way we both use and are used by them. We come upon an object that evokes thought within us because of its integrity, so the object and the thought arising become inseparable from one another.

I will now trace the development of my concept of the *evocative object* in order to consider it within this context.

The psychically valuable experiences of the day – those that compete to get into the dream that night – will contain islands of thought arising out of our experience of singular objects. Those objects leave an imprint in our unconscious that is partly the property of the thing-itself and mostly the result of its meaning within our individual self. If any of these experiences is unusually evocative it will, according to Freud's model at least, 'drive a shaft' down into the self's unconscious, where it will join existent and moving lines of thought.

But this shaft works both ways.

Shafts of interest

There are shafts of interest that emerge directly from our unconscious lines of thought to seek out and find specific things in our world that are objects of interest. I may have an impulse to go to an Arsenal football game because it fulfils an unconscious wish to have that experience. What it means in the chain of ideas running along in my mind at that time – out of sight of consciousness – I will not know. But I might just do it. Other experiences, however, will be tinged with anxiety, or sadness, or any one of the entire range of feelings we possess. We may not know why we feel the impulse to do something out of the blue, but it will no doubt have been at the behest of our unconscious, driving a shaft into our consciousness and giving us a directive.

As I discussed in *Being a Character*, during the day we are involved in ordinary dream-work, knitting together experiences in the real that form the tapestry of that day's unconscious meaning.[48] Actual things play a huge role in that dreaming, and this may be due to what they contain (mnemically), or how they function (their structure), or what enduring them will put us through (their processional integrity).

Free association, then, is a process that takes place both in the purity of the internal world and in the sullied world of actual things. Our movements in the mind and our meanderings in the real are certainly different action-categories. If we remained indoors for days – or weeks, or months or years – we would find our minds losing their food for thought. Emily Dickinson, perhaps our most famous poet–recluse, lived for a long time on the nurturing power of the order to be found in the poetic form. Eventually, however, that form decomposed in her intelligent hands as she lost the holding force of linear thinking and, as Helen Vendler illustrates, she moved around in increasingly crazed circles.[49]

We need contact with actual objects and we need lived experience. I do not know how many times I have said to analysands that they should allow experience to come and have its say in the outcome of their deliberation, before deciding in advance what they think about it!

Inner mental life and lived experience in the real are, of course, inseparable. Yet we can note how one's meandering in the real – moving from thing to thing – can in itself be a form of reverie that constitutes thinking in the real. Although such units of lived experience will evoke immediate unconscious meanings that link up to other chains of ideas, nonetheless the source of that psychic moment will be from the real and will carry the weight of the real with it *down* into the unconscious. Thought that evolves out of lived encounters in the real – juxtaposed to thoughts arising purely from mind alone – bear the marks of life.

The term 'evocative object'

At least since the Renaissance we have found ourselves increasingly free to comment on our own individual responses to evocative objects. As Masaccio brought ordinary human beings and objects to life in his paintings, he knew that his viewers would, in turn, find his renderings individually moving. The days of received meaning were on the wane as the Western world returned to the mysterious realm of human sensibility. Petrarch, looking back on the early Middle Ages, would declare that we were in a new 'modern' world, one in which man's search for human meaning was at least as important as his capacity to find his soul and send it on an everlasting journey.

Different poets and novelists obviously found different objects more evocative than others. For Wordsworth, it would be the countryside of his childhood. It may appear that he is simply describing an idealised pastoral landscape until one discovers, in *The Prelude*, that Wordsworth was using the evocative objects of his youth to examine the nature of thought itself. The subtitle of *The Prelude* is 'Growth of a Poet's Mind'. In evoking objects from his childhood, Wordsworth bears witness not simply to memory, but to the structure of imagination. His poem is meant to show his readers not only how contemplation of the object world is mind-expanding but how his own craft – poetic expression – grows along with the task of representation.

In *Moby-Dick*, when Melville puts Ishmael before a painting in the Spouter-Inn, he explores how unexpected encounters are mind-expanding. Ishmael sees a large oil painting that was 'besmoked, and every way defaced'. It had 'unaccountable masses of shades and shadows' and required viewing and reviewing before it began to make some visual sense. But what puzzled Ishmael the most was 'a long, limber, portentous, black mass of something hovering in the centre of the picture' which seemed 'boggy, soggy, squitchy'. After many attempts to define its subject matter Ishmael concludes that it is a whale impaling itself on a ship.

It is rumoured that Henry Murray, a psychologist and avid Melvillean, was inspired to create his psychological test – the Thematic Apperception Test, or TAT – from this scene in *Moby-Dick*. If so, then Murray noted what is, I expect, clear to any reader today. Ishmael's encounter with the unknown object at the beginning of the novel is a sly aside from Melville to his reader: read on, read what you will; make of this novel whatever occurs to you. Any encounter with any powerfully evocative object, suggests the author, forces us to think and think again. And as his intuition may have had it, *Moby-Dick* – an apparently simple tale of whaling – will turn out to be a very challenging read indeed. Our way of thinking about whaling will never be the same again. Our minds have been pushed to think in a different manner, processed by an object (a novel) which, when encountered, will change our mental life.

Decades later, Proust would take this double dimension even further. Objects were not simply mnemic vessels holding a specific memory; his was a system of thought that allowed recollected objects to become the ideational background to a new form of thinking.

The term 'evocative object' was used in psychology to refer to the self's capacity to evoke an internal mental representation of an object. 'Evocative object constancy' became a familiar phrase, especially amongst developmental psychologists and ego psychologists, that indicated the capacity to sustain important mental representations.

In 'The Transformational Object'[50] I argued that objects could act like processes. A mother encodes in her thousands of ministrations an implicit theory of being and relating that constitutes part of what I termed 'the unthought known'. In *The Shadow of the Object* I argued that we needed to add another term to our understanding of unconscious processes: 'the receptive capacity'.[51] When we receive objects (and that includes human others, of course) such reception is evocative. At that stage in my writing, I used the term 'evocative object' in two senses: to denote external objects that evoked inner states of mind, and also that which was evoked purely from the internal world. My emphasis was less on actual things in the object world than on people and how they affected one another, especially how the analyst affected the analysand.

Living with things

In *Forces of Destiny* I shifted my focus to the actual object world and how, as we use it, we fashion an existence for ourselves:

In the course of a day, a week, or a lifetime we are engaged in successive selection of objects, each of which suits us at the moment, 'provides' us with a certain kind of experience, and, as our choice, may serve to articulate our idiom, recall some earlier historical situation, or foreclose true self articulation.[52]

We do not know why we choose objects, but certainly one reason is because of their 'experience potential', as each object provides 'textures of self experience'.

Here I moved closer to the qualities of the object-as-thing. When I wrote that we 'need the object to release our self into expression'[53] I was acknowledging the intrinsic capacity of a singular object to do this. This was an essential feature of what I termed 'the destiny drive' and, in something of an elegiac mood, I wrote of how after one passes away we leave behind 'personal effects': the trace of those objects we used in our life that fulfilled (or perhaps did not) the needs of that drive.

The core of my theory at that time was that through actual object selection and use we could realise – that is to say, set free – our true self to its own idiomatic livings:

> The fashioning of life is something like an aesthetic: a form revealed through one's way of being. I think there is a particular urge to fashion a life, and this destiny drive is the ceaseless effort to select and use objects in order to give lived expression to one's true self.[54]

One of the gifts of a good enough mother or father is the providing of objects to one's child that meet the self's need for emotionally elaborating experiences. Objects presented in this way can be transformational and, being the object of the transformational potential of the other, they remain embedded within us for life.

> A person who meets up with a parent who is a good enough transformational object will have a sense of hope built into object use . . . and perhaps this is why a person has a sense of destiny.[55]

Through the chapter 'Historical Sets and the Conservative Process' in *Forces of Destiny* I argued that although we form screen memories, we also hold together sets of memories that serve to store self experience through the retentive power of the object. Although this essay emphasised our memories of past experiences within the object world, I also argued that children use objects in order to think:

Small children have a more intimate relation to concrete objects than do older children and adults . . . They think operationally by using objects, so the objects I remember are a part of my way of thinking about my life at the time.[56]

In *Forces of Destiny*, then, I aimed to show how it was actual object *use* in one's childhood – not simply thinking evocatively about an object – that inscribed itself in one's mind. Thus when thinking later of an object from one's childhood, one was implicitly recalling the experience of the object at the time. That temporal inscription was a crucial step in my turning to the view that it is the object as a thing-in-itself which needs the attention of psychoanalytic theory.

Impacts of the evocative

In *Being a Character* I argued that we needed now to study 'the structural effect of an object's impact on the self', and I wrote: 'I have found it rather surprising that in "object relations theory" very little thought is really given to the distinct structure of the object which is usually seen as a container of the individual's projections.'[57] I had no intention, of course, of discarding the way in which objects do serve as receptacles of the projected, but I was turning my attention now to the specific character of an object. Each object had its own integrity and came with its own 'processional potential'.

The object world 'is an extraordinary lexicon for the individual, who speaks the self's aesthetic through his precise choices and particular uses of its constituents'. In order to give full credit to the specific processional capability of an object, I wrote: 'Each thing in the lexicon of objects has a potentially different evocative effect by virtue of its specific form which partly structures the subject's inner experience and constitutes the eros of form in being.'[58]

In the second chapter of *Being a Character*, titled 'The Evocative Object', I attempted to outline how and in what ways actual objects affect the self. 'Living our life inevitably involves us in the use of objects that vary in their individual capacities to evoke self experience,' I wrote, emphasising the difference between objects. Objects possess a 'use-structure', I explained, as 'the employment of any particular thing brings about an inner profile of psychic experience specific to its character.'[59] It was important to conceptualise how each thing has its own profile.

Objects are also 'conceptually evocative'. Inspired in some ways by Lakoff's concept of 'categories of the mind' we can argue that an object will not simply belong to a category but will bear its concept. A food processor will carry within it the concept of food preparation, dining, relating to others through the sharing of food, and so on. In 'The Evocative Object' I argued that objects affect us in six ways: sensationally, structurally, conceptually, symbolically, mnemically and projectively. Although I might express this differently now, my aim was to explore the many sides of the actual object in our object world. While acknowledging that all objects have a mental place in our minds and are subject to mental metamorphosis, in directing attention to 'the structural integrity' of the object I intended to show how 'its atomic specificity' has a 'specific use-potential so that when it is employed it affects us in a manner true to its character.'[60]

I emphasised how our selection of objects, like our choice of words, is a means of our expression. But this works two ways: 'objects use us, in respect of that inevitable two-way interplay between self and object world.'[61]

Finally, by discussing how each object has a 'processional effect' I sought to link thinking with experiencing, or rather, how experiencing the object is a form of thinking.

The integrity of objects

In *Cracking Up* I continued my discussion of the integrity of objects by arguing that there is a developmental step beyond the infant's and child's use of the transitional object. We develop a 'separate sense' based on our use of actual things. 'The individual unconscious recognizes that any one object has a specific structure that makes its use for the subject transformationally distinct.'[62]

As we come to know this, we appreciate the specific integrity of an object: 'For the person who has begun to use objects to elaborate and articulate the self, *life is now considered as an object*. It is the next step after discovery of the transitional object.'[63] People who realise this emotionally have a deep appreciation of the object world in its own right.

Aesthetic dejection

In Chapter 2 above, we discussed how the built world exudes differing spirits of place. I want to turn my attention now to a form of depression that we might think of as 'aesthetic dejection'. It involves an irresolvable mismatch between self and object.

We all come across objects that we find off-putting at first. I did not like Mahler's music when I first heard it in the late 1950s but, after persevering, I found by the mid-1960s that I had fallen in love with his work. We all have these sorts of struggles with certain objects, and the struggle itself is an essential part of the growth of the mind.

Yet there are situations in which no matter how hard one tries, or for how long, it becomes clear that a certain object is just not usable. When we are unable to use the object or its processional potential, the object is evocative only in the sense that it gives rise to a form of dejection. I have tried and tried over the years to listen to heavy metal music and it is now clear to me that I will never turn the corner on this object. The mere sound drives me away. The same is true of certain cities. I know many people love Copenhagen and I have probably visited the city 15 times over the last 30 years, but each time I find it unappealing. I can point to certain things in particular that I do not like, but that is not the point: when it comes to Copenhagen and me, I cannot use this object. It depresses me.

Aesthetic dejection refers, then, not simply to the self's inability to make use of the object, but to a form of depression that the self knows cannot be resolved. The only solution is to be removed from the object itself.

But what if that object is the city in which one lives? What if I were assigned to live in Copenhagen? It is a mistake to assume automatically that the reason for such depressions is entirely intrapsychic. It may be, but it may not. Sometimes it is important for the person who is dejected to have his or her rejection of that object acknowledged as a thing-in-itself.

John Byng-Hall, the famous psychoanalyst who worked for decades at London's Tavistock Clinic, is reputed to have said that any good marriage is 'built upon hundreds of small marriages'. This has always struck me as one of the great pearls of wisdom in the clinical world. I do think that the best marriages, partnerships and friendships rely upon many small links between the two parties. Sometimes, however, one observes marriages that are clearly mismatches. And although it is true that 'opposites attract' – and in difference there may be freedom for a couple to enjoy that difference – if the difference applies to all realms of lived experience then, in most couples at least, we find a form of marital breakdown that I believe to be irreconcilable.

Such couples can plough on in a state of aesthetic dejection until they die, with nothing in common but shared misery and hatred – something that can be remarkably binding. Although each will no doubt point to endless shortcomings in the other, if they are to escape from their predicament they will need to understand that their dejection does not derive from personal failures. They are simply not a match, and the despair they feel is due to an irresolvable dejection.

This dejection à deux is not easily analysed; as such, patients are usually repeating the relational mismatches prevailing in their early childhood. When this is the case, the couple are wedded to an earlier failure and, in the sometimes curious logic of the repetition compulsion, they may feel impelled to remain in relation to one another as a form of binding and mastering something from the past.

Couples who share this dejection, however, do often appear in analytical consulting rooms when they enter elderhood. Ageing has a strangely sobering effect on the omnipotence of any conviction, and also on the power of repetition. In elderhood our individuality becomes increasingly obvious to us, just as we are becoming aware of our increasing dependence on the care of others. It is at this time in a life that a person – to the surprise of friends and family – can decide to opt out of a very long marriage. The reason? There is a depth perception of death heading one's way. In this respect death has, ironically, a liberating effect on the living. It can release them from other forms of death to live the last years of their lives in newly discovered forms of freedom.

Thinking *through* things

Conscious reasoning is a highly favoured form of thought, but within the fields of consciousness alone there are hundreds of ways to think. And when we include unconscious thinking in the mix, the doors open to an astonishing variety of thought systems. In the preceding chapters we have seen how, when we walk about in our world, we are poised at the intersection of two evocative objects: one purely internal, arising out of desire or affect, the other consisting of actual things we encounter in the real.

In my earlier works I have sought to extend Winnicott's concept of the 'use of an object' to argue that our encounter, engagement with, and sometimes our employment of, actual things is a *way* of thinking. As I amble through the department store, I might happen to catch the sports section out of the corner of my eye. I am not sure what I will find there, nor where exactly I will linger. I may pick up a hunting knife, have a look at it, then pass on to the baseball bats, and then move to the ping-pong tables. I am unlikely to be aware that in encountering these things I am actually engaged in thinking.

Life in this *form* of thought is picaresque. Like all people, I am on the move, travelling through the culture of objects, each bearing its own network of signifieds (a hunting knife for skinning a deer, for remembering Daniel Boone, for cutting up carrots, and so on) so that my day is lived according to this form of thought, as well as conscious thinking of various types, and many forms of unconscious thought.

Free association, then, is not simply the movement of ideas in our mind – jumping from one thought to another (whether spoken internally or reported to the other): it is also a movement of action. When moving in the real, the manifest contents of my meanderings are constituted out of the actual things I encounter. Any latent content will emerge from the aleatory vector as this thinking involves me in encountering the unexpected, out of which a type of thinking arises. Such existential thinking – born out of the necessity of immediate engagement with objects in the real – may in fact be one of the earliest forms of thought. Consciousness is at a minimum, so movement is accelerated due to the lack of reflection.

The ability to move freely in the object world, to use its thing-ness as a matrix for thinking-by-action, pivots around whether the aleatory object determines us – whether we move on quickly due to the dynamic of our last encounter with the object – or whether we select objects because we are unconsciously grazing: finding food for thought that only retrospectively could be seen to have a logic.

Either way, whether we are pushed to thought by objects arriving or we seek objects to use them as forms of thinking, it is clear to all of us that such existential engagements are a very different form of thinking from that of cognitive thought.

In a later work I hope to turn attention to the study of human character, which operates in the realm of action–thought. Driven by the idiom of our own self (our form of being) we select and react to objects in typical patterns of behaviour. When character is *thought about* it will usually be by others who have been *impressed* by the mark of the subject's idiomatic stamp. We ourselves become, then, evocative objects – living things – that bring about textures of inner experience within the other. So our character is a form of action–thought expressed through the use of the object world, and it will be subjected to a second form of thinking when those who encounter us as evocative objects register us in the world of their inner experience.

4

The fourth object and beyond

John Rickman's seminal paper 'The Factor of Number in Individual- and Group-Dynamics'[64] set both Balint[65] and Winnicott[66] to work on a psychoanalytic numerology. These days we assume that the number 1 refers to the self-alone, the number 2 refers to the infant–mother relationship, and the number 3 refers to the self's relation to the mother and the father. Each of these numbers suggests in the minds of psychoanalysts different psychologies: one-body psychology, two-body psychology and three-body psychology.

It can be argued that there is real clinical usefulness in considering which of these numbers is prevailing at any one moment in a session. This distinction may inform the sort of interpretations the analyst makes. If, for example, the analysand is talking about his wife, it might be presumed that the analyst is listening to the patient's work with the number 2. However, the patient may in fact be talking to a part of himself that he has projected into the wife. The patient is therefore working with the number 1 or, more aptly, indicating that there is something about being 'one of 1' that he cannot easily bear, so he resorts to creating a false second. In another example, a patient might be talking about a particular character dimension, such as his inability to think properly about what he regards as the more important issues of his life – apparently working with the number 1. In time, however, the analyst might discover that this point of view is the work of the other: that it reflects the projective identification of one of the parents.

Thus what looks like the patient's work in the area of the number 1 is in fact work with the number 2.

Assisting the psychoanalyst in the development of his or her psychoanalytic numerate sense will be the countertransference. The patient who is apparently talking about his own deficiency may evoke in the psychoanalyst an inner sense that what the patient is experiencing feels more like a sort of oppression. Thus the patient's affective turmoil surrounding this topic – indicated by his hesitations, his sudden grammatical breakdowns and so forth – seems to be the work of an 'interject', an internal object that has been projected into the self by the other.[67] The interject reflects the unconscious work of the other and sits inside the self, subject to very little unconscious elaboration, as it never constituted the desire of the subject in the first place. After a while, and shaped by the form of the analysand's transference, the psychoanalyst can therefore sense whether the issue being addressed by the patient is in the area of 1 or 2.

Our numerology is further complicated by psychic striation. A segment of time within a session may include work in all three numbers at the same time, segregated, not temporally, but by psychic function. So a patient might be talking to a part of himself (1), while simultaneously undertaking a dialogue with the mother (2) and also engaging in some conflict with the father (3). We might then wish to ask a Freudian question: which of these numbers bears the highest 'psychical value'? We could say that at any moment in time the entire numerology is present and engaged in some form of work, but from moment to moment one number intensifies in relation to the others. A patient talking about his wife may at one moment be discussing his own femininity, at another his unconscious attitude towards his mother's treatment of him, at another his sense of being the object of his father's desire. All three numbers, all three structures, are always present, but it is a matter of which number is the most active in any given moment.

It will be seen, naturally, that a psychoanalytic numerology bears no relation to mathematics proper. For example, we might say $1 + 1 = 3$. In psychic life there is one event which psychoanalysis must count in this way:

mother plus father produces a baby, which creates a three-some. But matters are considerably more complex than this for, as Lacan and others have argued, present in any sexual moment are each partner's parents. So in this respect the *experience of intercourse* may count as $1 + 1 = 4$.

But surely this actually adds up to 6: one partner plus two parents and another partner plus two parents? The logic here is that from the point of view of the number 1 who is experiencing it, there are in fact four people present. That is, in the psyche of one individual participant in intercourse there are the self, the sexual other, and the self's parents. (Intercourse *may* add up to 7 if we include the baby as one of the numerical figures.)

Couples on the verge of having their first child are beginning to assemble in their respective minds what it means to be *forming a family*. This includes many aspects. The couple search for the child's name. They fit out the baby's room and buy its first objects. In some countries they sign it up for a private school before it is born. They receive gifts from family and friends in anticipation of the infant's birth.

But in the system unconscious much more work is taking place than this. As the partners work their way towards forming a family, they begin the long and complicated task of constructing a shared object: we shall assign this the number 4. Gradually, thing-presentations are gathered in the unconscious around this fourth object.

From a psychoanalytic perspective we find a psychic numerology that not only does not add up, but also multiplies in complexity each time another element is added. This problem is produced by the fecund effect of sexuality upon psychic numeracy: as we can see, $1 + 1$ in the sexual addition does not add up to 2, but actually makes 3, and creates the possibility for 4. Thus 1 stands for the self, 2 stands for self and other, 3 stands for the procreative after-effects of sexual intercourse, and 4 stands for the family.

But wouldn't 3 already be the family? And isn't it an odd way to describe the birth of a child, as 'the procreative after-effects of sexual intercourse'? When a couple copulate and the after-effect is a child, we cannot assume that they form a family. For the family to 'arrive', further addition is necessary. There are many more elements contributing to the forming of a family than simply the arrival of the prospective family members.

Not every family can count to 4. Take, for example, the case of Isobel and James. They have intercourse and the after-effect is Jill. Isobel has never loved James, and she gives him his marching orders before the birth of Jill, who is then given up for adoption. In this case, although the child is born, the family is not.

Harry and Jessica

Harry and Jessica were childhood sweethearts, having grown up on the same street. Harry's father committed suicide when he was five and his mother – left with three young children – became severely depressed, took to drinking spirits, and was hospitalised for the first of many admissions when Harry was nine. Harry was looked after by his mother's brother, but the uncle hated him and subjected Harry to severe beatings until he reached mid-adolescence. Jessica's mother, meanwhile, had been married twice before and had had six children before Jessica was born. A born-again Christian, Jessica's mother was extremely exacting and devout in a misguided way, demanding that the children 'do without'. When Jessica was 11 her mother began to have visions of Jesus visiting the home and one day heard Jesus say that she must strip naked and walk down the middle of the street as a form of prayer. This she did, whereupon she was hit by a car and severely disabled – a shock to her life that she met with stony silence and a refusal to do anything but sew quilts for a Christian Aid store in the village where they lived.

During these years Harry and Jessica would come across one another frequently, but they never played together – they merely spent blank time in each other's presence. When Harry's uncle ran off and his mother was hospitalised once again, Harry dropped out of high school and moved into a neighbour's garage. Jessica helped him get hold of some of the things he needed. One day, that seemed to be Jessica; and they fell deeply in love when they were both 17. They moved into a large Chevrolet Impala, where they slept, ate fast-food meals and tried to put a life together.

Eventually they moved from their home town and travelled to California, where they both found jobs. Then problems began to arise in their relationship. They seemed to have little ability to tolerate each other's imperfections, and they could not talk these problems through. Both had psychotic episodes; Harry turned to crack cocaine; and although they lived together, to all intents and purposes they were no longer a couple.

Harry and Jessica had talked about having a family. This had served as an important object of conversation, but to the counsellor who eventually saw them – when in their late twenties – it was very clear that they had no idea what 'family' actually meant. We might say that in their case the fourth object was an aspiration considered from a standpoint of -1.

I shall use -1 to identify a position within psycho-analytic numerology that follows from Bion's concept of $-K$. Where K stands for knowledge, $-K$ stands for a mental state organised to rid the self of what it knows. Anyone approaching his or her future from a position of -1 will only accumulate further losses.

And $-1 + -1 = -2$. The more that Harry and Jessica talked about their life and their future, the more they added to their own subtraction. In five years they were so full of psychic losses, with each attempted addition only adding to their woes, that they had to give up on each other in order to try to start again. As Harry put it: 'We must cut our losses.'

In psychic numeracy, the concept of -1 identifies a position in which the self is less than 1. To be less than 1 (or even, to quote Brett Easton Ellis's title, *Less Than Zero*) is to have so many parts of the self missing that the self does not add up. It does not add up to 1. Such is the fate of the psychotic individual, and in thinking of Harry and Jessica – both of whom were brought up by psychotic parents and both of whom were divested of important parts of the self by the work of their own psychotic mechanisms – we may see how psychic losses can lead to a form of adding-up that serves only to make further losses inevitable. For if the mind cannot add in the first place, then any attempted addition will ultimately subtract from the solution, and the self will be left with a never-ending loss.

Counting to four

We could think of many situations in which intercourse and its after-effects do not create a family. We have seen that with the arrival of a baby, $1 + 1 = 3$, and that in order to create a family there must be a further addition. Out of these three people another object is formed. It is the first interpersonally constructed, vital, shared object that serves the function of opening lines of communication between its participants, in order that the family may be created. If one partner in the couple cannot count to 4, then even if the other partner can, and even if they go on to have many children, we can say that they have not been able to construct the fourth object: they will not have become a family.

Psychotherapeutic work with the family, whether in family therapy, in group therapy with couples, or in individual psychoanalysis with the patient's transference of the family, often reveals deeply painful failures of groups of people who cannot count to 4. Of course, with a psychotic couple – a Harry and a Jessica – it is very clear that no family can be created, and we bear witness to the awful realisation that psychosis must inevitably subtract from life. They might try to make false additions, but in time their losses will show up on the psychic accounts sheet.

But the more common anguish psychotherapists face is the group of three, or more, people who live together and who have in one way or another struggled mightily to form a family but have failed. Jim, for example, was in analysis. He had almost no memories before the age of 13. He was thoughtful and relatively insightful and his initial apparent amnesia was puzzling. He was quite able to tell himself about his mother, his father and his three sisters in my presence. However, I realised that Jim was describing individuals who were part of a group but who had never formed a family. Thus Jim's family memories were recollections of the group – but not remembrances of the family.

What is a family?

So what, then, is a family? What is that additional integer that makes 3 into 4? It is the integer that arrives only when the group has *created* the space for the fourth object to show up – a psychic object that serves the thing-presentation called 'my family' that will, in itself, act as a form of intelligence in the unconscious communications between the members of the group.

A family, then, is a special evolution in the history of the unconscious.

Indeed the history of the word 'family' reflects an evolution in the unconscious itself. According to the *Bloomsbury Dictionary of Word Origins*, the word 'family' comes from the Latin *famulus*, meaning servant.[68] From this was derived *familia*, which referred to the domestic servants in a household and their employers. It was introduced into English in its original Latin sense and so it survived until the end of the eighteenth century; but by the seventeenth century it had also widened in its usage to mean the whole household. Finally it narrowed to indicate 'a group of familiar people'.

So we come to 'familiar'. The *Bloomsbury Dictionary of Word Origins* tells us that 'familiar' originally meant 'of the family' and, intriguingly, its most common usage referred to a familiar enemy or familiar foe – that is, an enemy within one's own household. It then broadened to mean 'intimately associated' and finally to 'well-known from constant association'.[69]

From this etymology we can see a progression: from a collection of people who form a group, to a group of people who become 'intimately associated' with one another, that is, who become familiar with one another. An intermediate meaning seems to have been 'familiar enemy' – the enemy within the group. We may keep this as a question: does the fourth object have something to do with facing an enemy in a group, an encounter that adds to one's psychic economy?

The *Oxford English Dictionary* informs us that in the sixteenth and seventeenth centuries in England there was a sect called the Family of Love, originating in Holland, which had many followers – called 'familists' – and which 'held that religion consisted chiefly in the exercise of love, and that absolute obedience was due to all established governments, however tyrannical'.[70]

Let us imagine that emphasising love was a key psychic act in the formation of a family in order to establish a type of mentality that could process conflict with one's family enemies. For the *Oxford English Dictionary* then provides us with the following associated meanings:

> *happy families. Holy Family. in a family way* – in a domestic manner; informally. *in the family way* pregnant. *of family* – descended from noble or worthy ancestors. *'family'* (slang) – the thieving fraternity. *'The members of the family'* – a local organizational unit of the Mafia.

And what about the Mafia family, with its criminal connotations? Here we have family created not as an act of love, but as a group bonded together by blood in a different sense. Indeed the Mafia family engages in war with other families and directs hate existent within its own household into the outside world. Under no circumstances must anyone within the family betray the blood relation that forms the group.

This would allow us to insert the Freudian concept of the unconscious as memory. Thus our unconscious life recognises family, even if we do not consciously do so in ourselves. Perhaps this is why Freud played on the German word *unheimlich* (literally, 'un-homely') in his essay on the uncanny, finding that the uncanny is actually the unconscious familiar.[71] It is the self's arrival in a situation which is unconsciously known without being consciously comprehended.

Love law

When we think, then, of the group's construction of the number 4, we may come to an intermediate conclusion (a subtotal): that a group of people come together and face the common enemies intrinsic to group life by belief in the power of love as a form of law, which intermixes with the everydayness of this group to effect a type of informal intimacy with one another. This informal intimacy – the many, many shared moments – evolves out of this law of love and becomes a type of psychic structure that serves as the family's memory. In other words, a set is established in the system unconscious that we could condense into the following word-cluster: group–sex–blood–rivalry–love law–informality–intimacy–memory.

'Time and intercourse have made us familiar', wrote Samuel Johnson.[72] In the Freudian order, we might rearrange this into 'sex plus time has made a group familiar'. The after-effects of sexuality, blood, rivalry, love law and intimacy have combined, and the structure of family is in place.

Of course, the meaning of this cluster has behind its evolution the entire dramaturgy of the family imagined in Aeschylus, Sophocles and Shakespeare and, before that, in the imagining of the Old Testament. There one finds the group seeking to propagate itself yet torn by envy, rivalry and the forces of the death instinct, seeking to impose a new law – the law of love – that would serve as the eroticism of the group as a whole.

Love law is a vital part of the fourth object. The law that says 'thou shalt love thy neighbour as thyself' is an ancient edict which we may now look back upon as part of the history of the unconscious, an early stage in the formation of what we know as family.

Part of the structure of these dramas concerns a decisive moment: whether it is a man deciding to sacrifice his son to his god, a father deciding between his daughter's survival and his duty as king, or the decision to travel to a city on a certain fateful day when one's unknown father also takes to the road. These examples may be highly dramatic, but this structure is intrinsic to the formation of family. We may say the structure is the *moment of decision* when the self must choose between two opposing elements; when, in an extreme situation, the self is torn between deep loyalties. In terms of our discussion here, this would be the moment when two people come together to *decide* to form a family.

The formation of a family means the creation of a group that will unleash primitive internal forces that may tear it apart, unless the powerful law of love can impose itself sufficiently upon the group to see it safely through to the development of a new psychic structure, a memory-set composed of good enough experience lived together.

Marrying to kill

Each couple desiring to form its own family, however, does so in unconscious murder of their families of origin. Though they may come together to create new blood, blood is on the hands of the new couple. The symbolic fact of this murder is of course ritualised in the various marital ceremonies, in which parents give their children away. The unconscious sense in each couple that in marrying they have murdered their parents is, of course, one of the many after-effects of the Oedipus complex. Out of this ordinary matricide and patricide, the new children assume the right to sleep in the space of propagation. This is not merely the space of copulation, but the place from which the new family is to emerge.

Yet it is merely a foretaste of many things to come. For this *decisive moment*, when each partner must make an impossible choice – one that results in the death of a loved object – is only the first of many murders at the crossroads. Both partners bring with them the myths, legends, historic facts, laws, visions and aesthetic drives of their own families of origin. Some of these elements will be conscious and can be discussed, but all of them will also be deeply rooted in the self's unconscious life, forming a thing-presentation that we can see as the self's unconscious relation to its fourth object.

Both partners in the couple therefore bring to the relationship their previous experiences of family. These constitute fourth objects within. In some sense they will feel that in marrying they are killing the family of origin. This murdering is a deeply essential act of destruction, as both participants dismiss prior fourth object constituents in order to sustain a new fourth structure, and allow psychic intercourse between elements in the new family that are essential to fourth object life.

So the homicidal aspect that pervades the notion of family life is not simply the effort of the group to process rivalries emerging from its formation: it is a psychic after-effect of the decision to mate. This is the sexuality of homicide-propagation, of killing in order to give birth. Family life therefore begins in the unconscious with a primitive homicide, and the question is: can the couple survive what it has done? In the weeks and months following the marriage there will be many crossroads. Where to live? In what kind of house or flat? Furnished with what sorts of furniture? Decorated in what style? What sort of communication happens during the day, over what, and how? Arranging meals and dining in what idiom? Sexual life and the erotic in what differing elaborations? And the children that are coming: what names, what schools, what ideals, what visions, what . . . ? These are only a few of the many crossings of the new Oedipal couple on the road to Thebes.

Memories are made of this?

In each of these unconscious negotiations the murder of the families of origin is remembered. And yet the memories of previous times, too, are laid down as unconscious structures. So how do these structures deal with one another? Can there be a reintroduction of the families of origin, an after-copulation-intercourse in which the two sets of fourth objects negotiate their new positions?

Husband: I like coffee first thing in the morning.
Wife: I prefer tea.

> *Husband:*   Well . . . it's a bit much to make both at the
> same time . . . We're too busy.
> *Wife:*   I agree. Why don't you try tea for a while?
> *Husband:*   Okay, no big deal.

After a while the husband has not only made the transition
to tea, but now prefers it to coffee. In the years to come,
having breakfast with his sons and daughters, they will all
be drinking tea. This is no big deal, fortunately. Hardly the
sort of thing to work its way into Sophocles or Shakespeare.

Yet at this crossroads the husband's and wife's fourth
objects have met and one element in one set is killed off.
The husband, whose father and mother and brothers and
sisters always had coffee in the morning, abandons this
practice. The wife, in turn – in unknowing turn – agrees to
his request that the toothbrushes be put in a glass next to
the basin, brushes facing up. The wife has always had her
toothbrush in a fitted slot in a rectangular container, but
she thinks of this as unimportant and soon it is no longer
consciously occurring to her. When the children come, she
buys them a mug for their toothbrushes.

The holy family

In countless acts of unconscious murder, then, each partner
allows elements of his or her fourth object to be killed. This
is a sacrificial murder, one that allows the self to *lose the
familiar*. In time, the family of origin becomes a *holy family*
– sets of memories of the way things were. This holy family
– presided over by the holy ghost – is the original fourth
object, now simply a principle presiding over memories.
What is now merely memory was actually a deep unconscious structure, but the murderous work of marriage has
resulted in a destructuring of some aspects of the original
fourth object and its substitiution through the many years
of its rebuilding. Of course, we know that nothing is lost in
the system unconscious and the original fourth object is not
abandoned as a thing-in-itself. But its status has been
removed. It has been displaced from being the only fourth
object, and it has been sent to a holy place in the mind.

After its murder, associated with sacrificial necessity, it goes to mental heaven where the self feels that it shall forgive itself its murderousness.

The transition facing any two people who make the momentous decision to marry is, of course, hazardous in the extreme. It is the most dangerous decision of a lifetime. For years and years both partners will be killing off each other's inner psychic constituents, in an act of rebuilding constituted of sexual lust and love. For it will be this primitive love between the two that becomes its own law, originally narcissistic, but eventually transfiguring into a law of a different type. Sex-love will metamorphose to love law as the couple survive their mutual destructions and find that self-sacrifice is a part of human intimacy. From this a higher principle derives and serves the couple as they proceed to bring forth children. They will be more primitive even than the sex-couple were, and they will need 'guidance' from the parents – love guidance. The parents will convey to their children that there is a law within the family, that the love of family, or the family as love, must preside over any individual claimant's private rights to vengeance, or over any child's horror over the arrival of a newborn sibling.

If the parents have successfully formed their own new fourth objects, a matrix composed in the dialectic of difference, then they will have a psychic structure in place that can be communicated to the children. The fourth object, which we may now term 'the family', is of course separately held in each person. Marital therapy illuminates how this object differs as a psychic structure within each partner. But the object recognises that. Indeed, the fourth object is a psychic space that opens out to the illusion that it is a shared internal object, one always open to dialectics of difference, and operating according to the essential ruthlessness which Winnicott describes in his seminal essay 'The Use of an Object and Relating through Identifications'.[73] But, however ruthless, it is not destructive of the rights of the other; the other is killed but the self accepts its own killing. The fourth object is a principle of ruthless creativity in which the self seeks the unconscious communications of all the others in the group who are unconsciously negotiating in this field.

A family of five are chatting just before dinner; John is 15 years old, Mary eight and Peter two.

Father: So . . . John, are you playing football tomorrow?
John: Yeah, can you come?
Father: Ah . . . I . . .
Mary: Mum, I thought we were all going to the seaside?
Mother: Well . . . John . . . what time is the match?
Peter: What's a match?
John: It's football, Peter, remember . . . I think it's at one or two or something.
Peter: Play? Play football?
Father: That would split the day in two.
Mother: Well . . . what's the weather going to be like tomorrow?
Father: I think it's going to be fine . . . I don't know . . .
Mary: Can Sue-Ellen come to the seaside too?
Peter: Ellen, Ellen, Ellen, Ellen . . . yeah!
Father: [*thinking out loud*] What should we do . . .
Mother: How about the seaside on Sunday?
John: That would be good for me.
Mary: Oh no, Mum, I told Sue-Ellen Saturday!
Mother: You told her already?
Mary: Well . . . I thought you said . . .
Father: Well . . . Let's call her mother and ask if she can come on Sunday, and if she can't, then . . . What are we up to next weekend?
[*And so it goes on.*]

The family is engaged in trying to solve a simple spatial–temporal problem. All the members are taking part, although from differing points of view and with various unspoken conscious ideas – not to mention countless unconscious 'disseminates'[74] evoked by this moment in time. The family does not break down into malignant discord, because each member is not simply functioning as a member of the group, although that is also true, but is involved in object relations structured by the fourth object. Yet Peter is clearly clueless about this object and Mary and John are still involved in their individual formations of it, so how could we say that the family is functioning according to this psychic structure?

For a long time, in the early evolution of the new couple and then throughout the psychic formations of the growing children, this object exists in primitive form as a law: the love law. Because we love each other, this law goes, we get along. It does not mandate that we *must* get along. That would be the law of the group, but not the law of the family. The family law invokes 'blood' or its psychic equivalent, to form a more primitive assertion: as blood has brought us together, so we love each other, and this love asserts its law over all of us. It is the law that derives out of the Oedipal conflict, out of a set of murders that leaves all the participants with blood on their hands, yet blood-connected by intercourse. It is an extremely primitive form of transitional order. But it often works.

In the domestic scene portrayed above, the family members know in different ways that this law prevails. Even if one of the children had run off in tears to their room and refused to go along with the family's decision, it would not have destroyed the fourth object – the principle that governs forms of unconscious communication between the members.

The fourth object

We can see it in the above scene, although only in a glimpse. The fourth object is that psychic structure which receives and transmits at the level of unconscious communication the differing unconscious interests of members of the family group. It is governed, as we have seen, by a primitive law of love that serves to stave off primitive forms of hate in the children, long enough (usually) for the children to mature and then to cultivate an internal structure that operates less primitively. In time the children will feel the inner benefit of such openness. They will derive internal nourishment from this object that has survived personal distress

how fortunate are these people
and how absent any provision for the solitary

within the group – including moments of intense hate – and will come to appreciate consciously the unconscious benefit of knowing how to be open to the dialectics of difference in the group.

Of course we know that in the modern world many families have other qualifying elements that further complicate matters. Second and third marriages often bring ready-made families or sets of previous families. Much then depends on the previous marriages and on the status of the various fourth objects in the children. If they have fourth object structures forming within them, then they have lived according to a law that suggests to them that love should prevail. This edict – the law of the family and the family as law – helps new members of prior families to mesh together. Murder has always been a feature of marriage. Sometimes former spouses may be targets of active hostility on the part of one or both members of the new family, but this is only a development, an acting out, of the underlying act of murder that constitutes family life.

Implicit in the fourth object is its own eventual structural dissolution. Curiously, this knowledge also informs its character, as one knows that however essential the existing structure may be to one's self, eventually it will be displaced and the self will go on. Thus the adolescent, looking to his or her future and the forming of new fourth objects, and the ageing self will know that their own status as fourth object progenitor will be eradicated by the new generation's homicide and eventually – most tellingly of all – by organic death. Indeed, families unconsciously know this; they meet at a generational intersection. The parents are walking down the hill towards their graves and the children are walking up the hill to the future crests of their lives. The generations pass each other again and again on this hill, and the repetition of this family hike increasingly informs the fourth object in each that something generationally prescient exists within and between them and, in turn, within and between themselves and all the other families who have lived in the countless generations that preceded them. The *Epic of Gilgamesh* and the Old Testament give ordinary humans incredibly long lives, seeming to live for many generations reaching far into the future. This captures the simple place of the single family, passing along a common route on the journey of man and womankind.

So what makes up the number 4? We have played with the idea of a psychic numeracy, available for psycho-analysts as they add things up when considering their patients, or try to account for where they are. We have argued that $1 + 1 = 3$, but that an additional integer is needed to make $1 + 1 = 4$. We are now suggesting that this additional integer is 'love law'. Only when the group of 3, the after-effects of sexuality, have added a primitive element, is the fourth object to be counted.

Five and six

For the social group, I like to use the number 5. However, I have already suggested that 3 is a group, so I shall have to qualify this: 3 only ever represents the after-effects of intercourse. Three people may be present, but in fact they are lost in their collectivity until, or unless, they become a family. But members of every family will find, even after they have counted to 4, that the addition of a new psychic number threatens the promise of the number 4 as a psychically efficacious container. This additional integer stands for the self inside the social group, which obeys the laws of psychosis, not the love law, and it is here that the self's attachment to the family can be destroyed.

But let us remind ourselves of what we mean by destruction in psychoanalysis. All of the integers remain in the unconscious, even if further additions supersede them and seem to destroy them. Numbers 1, 2, 3, 4 and 5 there-fore survive any combinations that would seem to add up to more. When the child goes off to school for the first time and discovers that he or she is inside a group that is not his or her family – and that does not know the ways of his or her family – the child is psychically shattered. As Bion teaches us, this group life follows basic laws operating along a psychotic axis – one certainly not processed by any self through his or her family. But the fecund life of the self's imaginary is more than the fourth object can bear.

As the child discovers he or she has a mind, as he or she invents many mothers and fathers, the child is no longer held within the comforting illusion that he or she is being looked after by his or her family of origin. By the time the child is four or five years old, he or she will have begun to form the structure that is the fourth object, that will communicate and receive communications made for family life. The fifth object will break the hegemony of this structure as a promise of all future mixtures of people: the illusion of family as the only assembly will be dispelled. But the fourth object structure and its elements will remain and will continue to be available for the self in the years to come, as it processes the generational act of family life.

The fifth object – life in the group – is 4 + 1: four plus that which is outside the family. This is a harrowing experience for all of us, and it is common enough for individuals to begin a secret subtraction when they encounter 5. They may pair, forming themselves up with another to complete a couple: hence $5 - 3 = 2$, ridding the self even of the third object, to resume life in the more comforting arms of the dyad. They may even retreat into 1, seeking refuge in daydreaming or a form of autistic functioning. Fortunately, however, most of us manage to keep on counting, and though each new psychic integer destroys the former number and eradicates the seeming sanctity of its structure, the new numbers – the new structures – may also cure the self of damage that has been inflicted.

Number 6 is the self's addition of his or her place in a 'universal order' when the self can find, in universal assumptions and laws of civilisation, a new unconscious set. Indeed, this helps the self to survive difficulties in all the prior combinations, but especially when dealing with the madness of the group. During the Holocaust, when many lost their belief in humankind, others drew strength from the sixth object, from memory of and relation to the aims and aspirations of the human order – or man's humanity to man. At any one moment in time the group, 5, may lose its grasp of 6. The Nazis lost an integer. But in such moments our memory of 6 – perhaps useless as an unconscious factor in the life of society – is crucial to our own psychic survival.

Notes/References

1 Freud, Sigmund, 1913. 'On beginning the treatment', *Standard Edition of the Complete Psychological Works of Sigmund Freud* XII. London: Hogarth Press, p. 135.
2 Lacan's idea that the unconscious functions as the true Other – the other within the self – is nowhere more evident than in free associative thinking. The rigorous emphasis placed upon the analysand's speech in the session is one of the most important contributions to psychoanalysis.
3 Freud, Sigmund, 1923. 'Two encyclopaedia articles', *Standard Edition of the Complete Psychological Works of Sigmund Freud* XVIII. London: Hogarth Press, p. 238.
4 Some psychoanalysts mistakenly assume that because they cannot follow their patient's line of thought, the patient must be attacking links between ideas. Some may even feel that their own minds are being assaulted. This unfortunately confuses links established unconsciously with links operating at the level of the manifest content. If one practises from the Freudian perspective, then one assumes that it will not be possible to follow the material in the here and now on a conscious level: indeed, attempting to do so refuses the very nature of unconscious communication itself. It is an indication of how far some psychoanalysts have drifted from the original paradigm of psychoanalysis that too many analysts require of themselves, their colleagues and their students the 'ability' to follow the patient's meaning in the here and now.
5 Freud, Sigmund, 1923. 'Two encyclopaedia articles', *Standard Edition of the Complete Psychological Works of Sigmund Freud* XVIII. London: Hogarth Press, p. 239.
6 Freud, Sigmund, 1915. 'The unconscious', *Standard Edition of the Complete Psychological Works of Sigmund Freud* XIV. London: Hogarth Press, p. 194.

7 Freud, Sigmund, 1912. 'Recommendations to physicians practising psycho-analysis', *Standard Edition of the Complete Psychological Works of Sigmund Freud* XII. London: Hogarth Press, p. 115.

8 For a discussion of how the psychoanalyst's unconscious distorts the patient's material and how this, ironically enough, itself constitutes unconscious communication, see 'Communications of the unconscious' in Bollas, Christopher, 1995. *Cracking Up*. New York: Hill and Wang, pp. 9–29.

9 In psychotic states, or when the patient is not free associating but engaged in a form of resistance, the psychoanalyst will not be able to use the part of the ego that is psychically evolved to follow the pattern of the other.

10 For an interesting discussion of the many differing 'listening perspectives' in psychoanalysis, see Hedges, Lawrence, 1983. *Listening Perspectives in Psychotherapy*. New York: Jason Aronson.

11 Heimann, Paula, 1956. 'Dynamics of transference interpretations', *International Journal of Psychoanalysis* 37, pp. 303–10.

12 See Bollas, Christopher, 1987. Introduction to *The Shadow of the Object*. London: Free Association Books, p. 2.

13 For a discussion of how free association constitutes a play of the mental lives of both psychoanalyst and patient, see Part 1 of Bollas, Christopher, 1987. *Forces of Destiny*. London: Free Association Books.

14 Hirsch, Edward, 1999. *How to Read a Poem*. New York: Harcourt Brace, p. 31.

15 Hirsch, *How to Read a Poem*, p. 146.

16 For further discussion of 'subject relations theory' see Bollas, Christopher, 1987. *Forces of Destiny*. London: Free Association Books.

17 Freud, Sigmund, 1911. 'The handling of dream-interpretation in psycho-analysis', *Standard Edition of the Complete Psychological Works of Sigmund Freud* XII. London: Hogarth Press, p. 94.

18 Freud, 'The unconscious', p. 190.

19 Freud, Sigmund, 1900. *The Interpretation of Dreams*, in *Standard Edition of the Complete Psychological Works of Sigmund Freud* V. London: Hogarth Press, p. 525.

20 See Freud, Sigmund, 1923. *The Ego and the Id*, in *Standard Edition of the Complete Psychological Works of Sigmund Freud* XIX. London: Hogarth Press, pp. 3–66.

21 See Bollas, Christopher, 1992. *Being a Character*. New York: Hill and Wang.

22 Breuer, Josef, and Freud, Sigmund, 1893–5. 'Studies on

hysteria', *Standard Edition of the Complete Psychological Works of Sigmund Freud* II. London: Hogarth Press, p. 289.

23 Breuer and Freud, 'Studies on hysteria', p. 290.

24 See Bollas, Christopher, 1974. 'Character: the language of self' in *The International Journal of Psychoanalytic Psychotherapy*, 3(4), pp. 397–418.

25 Freud, Sigmund, 1929. *Civilisation and its Discontents*, in *Standard Edition of the Complete Psychological Works of Sigmund Freud* XXI. London: Hogarth Press, p. 70.

26 Lynch, Kevin, 1960. *The Image of the City*. Cambridge, MA: MIT Press (1996), p. 5.

27 Montet, Pierre, 1958. *Everyday Life in Egypt in the Days of Ramesses the Great*. Philadelphia: University of Pennsylvania Press (1981), p. 18.

28 Bachelard, Gaston, 1958. *The Poetics of Space*. Boston: Beacon Books (1994), p. xvi.

29 Crawford, Harriet, 1991. *Sumer and the Sumerians*. Cambridge: Cambridge University Press.

30 Hersey, George, 1988. *The Lost Meaning of Classical Architecture*. Cambridge, MA: MIT Press (1995).

31 Lynch, *The Image of the City*, p. 5.

32 Bachelard, *The Poetics of Space*, p. xxiii.

33 Bachelard, *The Poetics of Space*, p. 8.

34 Lynch, *The Image of the City*, p. 45.

35 Lynch, *The Image of the City*, p. 42.

36 Winnicott, Donald, 1969. 'Berlin Walls', *Home is Where We Start From*. London: W.W. Norton (1986).

37 Lynch, *The Image of the City*, p. 1.

38 Bachelard, *The Poetics of Space*, p. 11.

39 Field, M., 1995. 'Classroom on stilts puts new life into an old prefab', *The Architects' Journal*, vol. 3, p. 23.

40 Barthes, Roland, 1964. 'The Eiffel Tower' (1979), *The Eiffel Tower*. New York: University of California Press (1984), pp. 3–22.

41 Winnicott, 'Berlin Walls', pp. 221–2.

42 This definition of the Situationists' concept of psycho-geography is provided by Harris, Steven and Berke, Deborah, 1997. *Architecture of the Everyday*. Princeton: Princeton Architectural Press, p. 20.

43 Dewey, John. *The Philosophy of John Dewey*, ed. John J. McDermott. Chicago: University of Chicago Press (1981), p. 561.

44 Dewey, *The Philosophy of John Dewey*, p. 555.

45 Dewey, *The Philosophy of John Dewey*, p. 556.

46 Dewey, *The Philosophy of John Dewey*, p. 557.

47 Bollas, Christopher, 2007. *The Freudian Moment*. London: Karnac Books, pp. 1–32.
48 Bollas, Christopher, 1992. *Being a Character*. New York: Hill and Wang.
49 Vendler, Helen, 2006. *Poets Thinking: Pope, Whitman, Dickinson, Yeats*. Cambridge, MA: Harvard University Press, pp. 64–91.
50 Bollas, Christopher, 1979. 'The transformational object', *International Journal of Psychoanalysis* vol. 60, pp. 97–107. Reprinted in Bollas, Christopher, 1987. *The Shadow of the Object*, London: Free Association Books, pp. 13–29.
51 Bollas, Christopher, 1987. *The Shadow of the Object*. London: Free Association Books.
52 Bollas, Christopher, 1989. *Forces of Destiny*. London: Free Association Books, p. 48.
53 Bollas, *Forces of Destiny*, p. 48.
54 Bollas, *Forces of Destiny*, p. 110.
55 Bollas, *Forces of Destiny*, p. 112.
56 Bollas, *Forces of Destiny*, p. 199.
57 Bollas, *Being a Character*, p. 4.
58 Bollas, *Being a Character*, p. 22.
59 Bollas, *Being a Character*, p. 33.
60 Bollas, *Being a Character*, p. 35.
61 Bollas, *Being a Character*, p. 37.
62 Bollas, Christopher, 1995. *Cracking Up*. New York: Hill and Wang, p. 88.
63 Bollas, *Cracking Up*, pp. 90–1.
64 Rickman, John, 1950. 'The factor of number in individual- and group-dynamics' in *Selected Contributions to Psycho-analysis*. London: Hogarth Press and the Institute of Psycho-Analysis (1957), pp. 166–7.
65 See Balint, Michael, 1968. *The Basic Fault*. London: Tavistock Publications, pp. 27–9.
66 See Winnicott, Donald, 1971. 'The maturational process and the facilitating environment: studies in the theory of emotional development' in *Through Pediatrics To Psycho-Analysis*. London: Tavistock (1958), pp. 135–8.
67 See Bollas, Christopher, 1999. *The Mystery of Things*. London: Routledge, p. 113.
68 Ayto, John, 2001. *The Bloomsbury Dictionary of Word Origins*. London: Bloomsbury.
69 Ayto, *The Bloomsbury Dictionary of Word Origins*, p. 218.
70 *Oxford English Dictionary*, online version (accessed 30 March 2008) of the second edition (1989). Entries for 'family', sense 7 and 'familist', sense 3.
71 Freud, Sigmund, 1919. 'The uncanny', *Standard Edition of the*

Complete Psychological Works of Sigmund Freud XVII. London: Hogarth Press, pp. 217–56.

72 Johnson, Samuel, 1751. *The Rambler* no. 160 (28 September 1751).

73 Winnicott, 'The use of an object and relating through identification'.

74 To coin a word, a 'disseminate' is a single particle of a dissemination. It would be a 'loose thread' from a former fabric, now constituting part of the self's disseminations of all prior psychic intensities that form an infinite meshwork in the system unconscious. A disseminate is thus any particle out of the dissemination of mental contents that is evoked by any new psychic event and attaches itself to it.

Index